Troubled Intimacies

Troubled Intimacies

A Life in the Interior West

David Axelrod

Oregon State University Press
Corvallis

The paper in this book meets the guidelines for permanence and durability of the Committee on Production Guidelines for Book Longevity of the Council on Library Resources and the minimum requirements of the American National Standard for Permanence of Paper for Printed Library Materials Z39.48-1984.

Library of Congress Cataloging-in-Publication Data
    Axelrod, David, 1958-
  Troubled intimacies : a life in the interior West / David Axelrod.— 1st ed.
    p. cm.
  Includes bibliographical references.
  ISBN 0-87071-038-9 (alk. paper)
  1. Axelrod, David, 1958- 2. College teachers—Oregon—Biography. 3. Poets, American—21st century—Biography. 4. Naturalists—Oregon—Biography. 5. Oregon—Biography. 6. Oregon—Social life and customs. 7. Landscape ecology. 8. Human geography. I. Title.
  CT275.A9524A3 2004
  979.5'043'092—dc22

2004010211

OREGON STATE
UNIVERSITY

Oregon State University Press
101 Waldo Hall
Corvallis OR 97331-6407
541-737-3166 • fax 541-737-3170

Contents

Acknowledgments

Grateful acknowledgment is made to the editors of the following publications in which parts of *Troubled Intimacies* first appeared, and sometimes in different form: *Cimarron Review, The Chronicle of Community, The Kenyon Review, Southern Poetry Review.* I would like to thank Eastern Oregon University for its generous support through the Summer Merit Scholars Program, and the Fishtrap Foundation for its support through the Imnaha Writer's Fellowship Program.

I owe my thanks also to Jodi Varon, Jo Alexander, George Venn, Donald Wolff, David Memmott, Craig Lesley, Robert Stubblefield, Debra Earling, Bob Ross, Sandra Alcosser, Peter Matthiessen, Hank Harrington, and Conrad Hilberry, all of whom have either encouraged or sobered me up in respect to my enthusiasms as I wrote this book. Any errors or infelicities in the text are entirely my own.

Going Wild

The Elkhorn Mountains aren't the landscape calendar photographers or tourists prefer; the Wallowas, east across the valley, are where crowds gather within the boundaries of a conventionally picturesque wilderness. The Elkhorns are not as high as the Wallowas; are drier, less geologically complex, and less diverse in terrain; and besides two fragments, are unprotected by wilderness boundaries. They are the site of a brief moment in the Oregon Gold Rush, and mining still goes on, though meagerly, crossed pickaxes dotting maps. What the maps do not depict are the scattered tailings piles, mine shafts, and ponds contaminated with heavy metals.

Having lived my early life far from the Elkhorns makes me, in the eyes of the descendants of early settlers, an interloper. To live at ease with the "traditional values" of northeastern Oregon means accepting as right and proper the violence that wounded these mountains. These are public lands, but "public" in name only, and the "right" to make a living off of this land is retained by those who arrived here in the second half of the nineteenth century. Nevertheless, my early experiences in the Ohio coalfields, where uplands and valleys vanished under tailings, causes me to feel oddly at home here, seeing clearly enough, despite my disreputable status.

The Ohio I was intimate with, an area running diagonally across the eastern third of the state from Nelson's Ledges to the Hanging Rock Iron Region, provided ore, timber to fire furnaces to smelt the ore, and later coal to fuel the heavy industry iron made possible. That former wilderness exhausted its resources, and today remains impoverished. No longer valued, the land is ignored, and wounds inflicted on it have begun the impossibly slow process of healing. I came of age walking at the edges of those wounds. In the Elkhorn Mountains, as in other areas in the interior Northwest, I walk at the margin of a peculiar violence. I have seen it before; its consequences are familiar.

❧❧

From Dutch Flat Saddle in the Elkhorns, it is a short descent to Cunningham Saddle, where the trail crosses the ridge and looks down on the headwaters of the North Fork of the John Day River. The upper reach of the watershed is a timbered valley—lawfully designated wilderness. Three miles farther downstream, however, logging and mining define its western boundary. Beyond those cut-over areas, parallel mounds of tailings line the stream until it disappears into a canyon, entering yet another portion of official (though fragmented) wilderness. Along ridges that surround the drainage are a familiar patchwork of clear-cuts.

Can such fragmented lands in any legitimate way be called "wilderness?" If not, landscape is reduced to an aesthetic perception; that is, wilderness defined only by our ability to look across a significant distance without any evidence of human intrusion, an illusion the western landscape in some places allows. Such a definition, however, condemns these fragmented lands to further neglect, even contempt.

Or we may concentrate on the near at hand, which is wild, "innocent" of such aggressive desires as logging or mining. Here in the Elkhorns, the intimacy of looking at the wild near at hand, the specific living being that refuses to abandon its place, becomes an awkward necessity, sole criterion for defining wilderness. Still, whenever I look up from the ground at my feet, contrasting shades of light demarcate the bounded wilderness and the landscape transformed by industrial uses that surrounds it. In some places, the wilderness boundaries are clear-cut surveyor-straight.

There are always more edges to the inviolate wild; ever more bounded territory where evidence of human intrusion cannot be forgotten much less ignored. But to long for a former world or pretend it still exists is a delusion. Ours is a world diminished by our aggressive inventions, and to deny that is to willfully participate in the ongoing crime against what intact landscapes remain. Our delusion is predicated on the notion of a receding frontier, and an ahistorical territory beyond that frontier; with enough dollars you may visit before it too is "corrupted" by modernity.

The lonely planet, with its five billion hungry human souls, is not lonely, and "unexplored territory" is nothing less than a ploy meant to appeal to the Romantic longings of the privileged. Few of us live in a place that remains anything like its remote, inviolate creation. Our world is more ambivalent and complicated, a place of broken light and shadow, observed only in contrasting, dissonant elements. Where I live is a landscape that, though it is not urban, is nevertheless wounded by industry, the flow of profits from which leads directly back to the cities that many contemporary rural (and urban) dwellers say they disdain. As though disdain of this sort were a crucible in which we are made pure. Does virtue accrue to us because we are willfully blind, disingenuously ashamed of the diminishing beauty of the natural world? Does such "virtue" exempt us from earth's judgment?

My former student, Jerry, was the child of a family that came into these northeastern Oregon mountains soon after arriving here in a wagon train. They homesteaded in the Baker Valley and for three generations mined claims just south of Summit Pass. He remembers how, on a lark, they would dynamite stream beds that once were full of salmon smolts from the sea-runs that spawned in the creeks on their claim. He remembers sunlight refracting through the spray, the heavy thud of boulders landing on moss, old ponderosas crashing to his and his father's and uncle's cheers of triumph. Before they destroyed those creeks, he recalls the water turned white with milt during the spawn. He grieves now over his participation in that greedy fantasy of quick wealth that never came. The numinous perfection of that earlier world he remembers the last moments of is lost; the scars of his passing through are visibly evident to him from many miles distant. He never returns to these mountains, never risks any intimacy; his own life seems strange to him now, and strangely impoverished.

Jerry has since moved to Kansas.

⚳

My family has lived in Ohio since the eighteenth century, and played an early role in its being raped, never asking whose land it was before we claimed it ours. Instead we told the story of hardship endured, the winter men quartered at Fort Defiance, waging Mad Anthony Wayne's Indian War. The women left behind at that edge of Ohio wilderness failed to gather the garden before an early freeze. Cows fell ill. Then children. Game grew scarce and famine walked back roads. An infant died. Perhaps others would die. Perhaps we were observed gouging out a grave in frozen ground.

Observed by whom? Wyandotte, Miami, Shawnee, Erie? She could have been any of them. The only word we had for her then as now is *squaw*, an insult. She appeared, a trick of sight, from forest across the field from our unpainted saltbox, a deer slung across her shoulders, and staggered over snow toward the door, my kin cowering below windowsills, loading muskets, giddy with imminence of battle. She laid the deer at the threshold. Where I have stood many times, listening to corn thicken in maniacal rows. Where I have caught only a glimpse of her absolute retreat across that field two centuries ago.

Who was she? Even if I knew—forests beaten back now into hollows, old trees gone, creeks fouled by mines and drifted deep with silt—would I dare offer her thanks? I wish to find an end to this legacy of cruelty, but wherever I walk, I walk the edge of a wound our history seldom permits to heal.

The Wrights farmed east of our homestead after the Civil War. A brother and sister, ex-slaves who found one another and for the remainder of their lives honored the primacy of blood. Our last memory of them is threshing time circa 1900. No one knows who buried them side by side in a plot at the back of their farm, a pasture overlooking woods that surrounded their cabin. All that remained of the Wrights' cabin was moss-covered limestone foundations grown up in vine maples and orange touch-me-nots I was taught to crush to soothe a rash.

Their forty acres became ours, though no record of sale exists. Thus we took possession of mineral rights to strip-mine that hillside, though no one bothered to scruple about the overgrown graves as lights from the big shovel shone above the ridge at night. We "reclaimed" the land afterward: leveled the hillside, trucked and bulldozed topsoil back into place with its cargo of human bones, right and proper for the sowing to soybeans and corn.

I once hurried across the sheep paddocks, climbed tailings replanted in parallel rows of white pines to a clearing overgrown by clumps of grass I knew only by the name "poverty grass." Thickets of sumac and blackberries teemed in the valley, scabbing over the flayed carcass of hills men had gorged on with their colossal machinery, hauling away coal. A kind of revelation sweated through the pores of my skin, a legacy that permitted no exceptions. The terrible gift of that land: healing, impudent, lovely. A mind going wild.

ℒℒ

We pretend that our relations to the land are somehow different in the western than in the eastern United States; the West is endlessly rich with possibilities: scenic, economic, spiritual, and all of these self-aggrandizing as the myths told about any frontier. We live as Romantics. One writer fantasizes about being the first explorer of the upper Snake River Valley, the first to walk under the Tetons. A feeling arises from that image of impossible, loathsome longing for a "virgin" world, a "true" wilderness, innocent of history. No such world existed. Only another people's way of living in relation to what we mistook for an uninhabited land. Wilderness is not a status we grant the landscape. It is earth's only way of being as it chooses. What it chooses to be is alive, and if cut to the quick, to knit itself again into a whole.

Let Romantics walk in isolate dreams of a static virginal world. I wish to walk only here, where what is alive is most thoroughly and undeceptively alive: these wounded mountains.

A Westward-Going Heart

Eight more years would pass before I moved to northeast Oregon. I first came west, however, as a student in Richard Hugo's last poetry workshops at the University of Montana, where I arrived in the summer of 1980, at the age of twenty-two. It is a rare and lucky moment for a young writer if he enters into a productive apprenticeship with his teacher. This was certainly not the case for me; I was too young and immature, too shy or too much in awe, and the learning was haphazard and awkward. Only later, when the relations between us ended altogether, did any learning occur. And although I found myself renting an ugly, paneled basement apartment in Missoula, and was eager to begin classes, if it had been required of me at the time, I would have been unable to explain why I wanted, much less why I needed, an MFA in creative writing. Besides the fact that I had written poems on a regular basis since elementary school and had published several in literary magazines while an undergraduate, I was an altogether poor prospect.

There was, however, no mystery about why I found myself in that basement apartment, beneath the French Canadian couple's living room, where nightly they resumed their long, bitter, and well-rehearsed quarrels.

As an undergraduate, I had gravitated early toward Theodore Roethke, drawn to his vigorous cadences, and his imagery of a damp, rich, chaotic earth. The wild and domestic collide in a celebratory awe. Soon, I followed the branching lines of descent among his students; chief among those was James Wright, a fellow working-class Ohioan, in whose poems I first heard something approaching the language of my own family's experiences in the small steel towns along the Mahoning River, only a few hours north of Wright's black swan of the Ohio. From Wright to Hugo, who I understood had been his classmate in Roethke's courses, was no great distance, despite the geographic distance between the scenes of their poems. Whatever their actual social views may have been, the working-class experience that was central to their writing seemed to me sympathetic to the poor and the powerless among whom I had spent my childhood. Even in despair and loneliness their personae operated from an original position that seemed to state: The world could be kinder, fairer, and more just. As a teenager reading their work I encountered for the first time the sad outrage at circumstances that their language gave shape to, as well as a promise that justice, if it existed at all, might originate in the economy of the words.

In their work I heard my first hint that the language of a poem may be simultaneously a moment of surrender and redress, as though all the psychological moorings to personal security must be undone before we might actually encounter the suffering of the world and perhaps begin to ease its grip on the lives of others. In their poems, I heard a voice for whom or what is vulnerable and voiceless. Toward each poet I felt a strong native allegiance. They expressed a conflicted but proud social identity. My sympathy for their work was a response to their evocation of the people and experiences familiar to anyone growing up in the by-then-dwindling industrial and agricultural working class of the Rust Belt.

In each of their bodies of work, there is—and I recognized this even as a teenager—an ever-ameliorative natural world, vanquished to the margins of human social pathologies, always encroaching, healing the harm inflicted on the earth and on ourselves. It is our responsibility to stand witness at the margins of those historical and industrial wounds. The natural world is a complex, sometimes benign reality, where, despite human intentions to the contrary, "the branch will not break." But the branch did break in the spring of 1980. James Wright died in March of that year in New York City, and it seemed obvious to me which direction my life would then turn.

I was not moving to New York City, but to Montana.

𝒬𝒬

The blackguard faction of my family in fact had already arrived in Montana decades earlier. They settled along the Clearwater and Snake rivers in the 1920s, then migrated farther west and north into Washington, Montana, and Oregon. The Montana clan—Weirs, Faulkners, and Millses—were not so clear about the lines of descent that joined us one to another, though they were curious to know just what sort of greenhorn named Axelrod from the East wished to settle among them. And with all the devotion that blood (even thin blood) demands, they prepared my way by renting me that basement apartment not far from Missoula's notorious Malfunction Junction, and kept me busy in the woods throughout the summer and early autumn of 1980—gathering pine cones to sell to the timber company, cutting firewood, and hunting bear, deer, and elk—so that I might have some spending money and food on the table.

Whatever stories they told about their eastern relatives they never shared in my presence. Perhaps they had no stories about us at all, as we had remained only the vaguest presence beyond the horizon of their world. All my life, however, I had heard stories about my grandmother's rogue brother, "Arthur, who went out to live among the wild Indians on the western frontier." His children, and their children, too, it was confided to me in a scandalized hush, were known to be "real mountain men." If these stories were meant as a caution against my being attracted westward, they had the opposite effect. A place was already set for me at the table among these people, who, excepting their economic situation, which was familiar to me, promised to be unlike anyone I had ever known. I delighted in my new status as a potential blackguard. I did not imagine myself in buckskins with a blunderbuss over my shoulder (though I soon would find such people did exist). I knew there would be pickup trucks aplenty, whiskey, rifles, bulldozers, hunting trips, wood gathering, and all of it in the Rocky Mountains. In Montana, I would be free to reimagine my entire life and wear whatever new mask I might choose.

Mountains were not the least important reason I found myself in Missoula. As much as anything else, the photograph on the front cover of the U of M Graduate Bulletin convinced me to forget about other, more prestigious schools that an ambitious young writer would choose to attend. The photo was taken from Mount Dean Stone: Missoula in the foreground below, and the snow-covered Rattlesnake Mountains and pine forests rising to the north. Looking at the USGS maps in the library back in Ohio, I realized that if I chose to, I could walk into those mountains and find my way over one hundred miles north to Canada, and cross only two roads, one of them dirt.

🌿🌿

When I arrived at the University of Montana in the fall of 1980, Richard Hugo was on leave, teaching at the University of Arkansas. Years later, a publishing rep would tell me the story of meeting Dick as he limped across the Fayetteville campus. To the book rep, Dick seemed out of place—wheezing, sweating, nonacademic in his demeanor. "I'm just here for a couple of months," he gasped. "I give them some readings, meet a few students, and they pay more than I make all year in Montana." Then Dick brightened and added, "Christ, it's nice work if you can get it." He burst out laughing at this—his mouth, I imagine, in its typical wide, toothy grin, his brow knit, and his whole body (it was an ample body at that time) shaking with merriment at his predicament.

William Pitt Root replaced Dick at the U of M that fall. I was still far too immature and lacking in social skills to benefit in any way from the workshops I would attend in the following two years. The apprentice poets, with a few exceptions, were older, by my standards anyway, in their late twenties and thirties, some even older. A few were already confident writers, grown men and women with well-established senses of themselves, and soon-to-be-published books. And my classmates were old hands in the workshop scene, something I was not. The night of our first class meeting, each student brought new work to read aloud. Everyone, that is, except for me and a few of the other bedazzled new students. I demurred when called upon, passing the torch of genius to the next poet, so as not to burn myself too soon.

It was a good thing, too, that Dick was gone—a fact I learned in embarrassing circumstances that first term. My adoration of his poetry was untempered. I brought two Ohio poems to the workshop early on, the titles of which give away the problem to anyone who has read Dick's poems: "Leaving Magnetic Springs," and "Photographing Orland." Today, I have no problem recalling the initial impulses of those poems, though I wrote them over two decades ago, and they have since disappeared into smoke and ashes. If anything, they were intended to be little more than summer images such as Charles Burchfield may have painted of a broken-down spa resort in the tawdriest years of its decline and an abandoned coal-mining town overwhelmed by the riotous green of the Appalachian foothills. I may have intended to write poems that were intimate, celebratory, and brief. But instead, I slipped on the familiar Hugo mask. They were unabashed imitations of Dick's own triggering town methods, an outright theft of his perennial outsider's stance, his melancholy voice, his focus on destitution, his bitter emotionalism, his consonant, variable iambic line. This was the single strategy I could imagine in order to sympathize with people in places and circumstances close to my home and experience. Such were the seductions of Dick's voice. It was ironic that I had ridden my bicycle almost one hundred miles to the site of each poem—I was an athlete, for Christ's sake, not a lonely, destitute dipso! After I had written these poems, it never occurred to me that these very distinctive elements of Dick's poetry were not exactly in the public domain. Assuming Dick's persona was so easy to do, but I wonder now at how it could overpower my own instincts. Whatever persona I may have invented independent of my absent mentor was still too fragile and amorphous to withstand the seductions of his mask.

I read "my" poems to the workshop. People laughed. I had not thought that they were funny poems. Then there was a silence in the room that lasted as long as unanaesthetized oral surgery. Finally, a student, Candace, explained as gently as possible that I was not going to do this sort of thing ever again. OK, I thought, that is easy enough. She began, however, to read individual lines as evidence of my literary crimes. Others joined in, and it soon became resident teaching day at St. Hugo's poetry hospital. It was an error I would never make again.

Although I did not know it at the time, I was a very lucky young fellow that night I read my parroted lines to the class. Others were less lucky. A year later, a student would make much the same error, but in Dick's presence. The student finished reading "his" poem and looked up satisfied at Dick, expecting praise for his lines that honored the style and methods of our teacher. Imitation is an essential element of apprenticeship; I do not believe that is in dispute here. Students of the old masters painted in the styles of their mentors, so as to confuse the actual "authorship" of a painting. My own friends in art school then were required to copy the work of their teachers, as well as the work of past and modern masters. William Pitt Root had advised us to write out other poets' poems by hand. James Welch's early poems sometimes shared more than the very same titles as Dick's poems; they shared as well Dick's familiar stance, style, and methods, even his vocabulary. And Dick's delight with Welch was well known, though this was not the case that day in our poetry workshop. Later, Dick would in fact tell us to imitate, since imitation was inevitably an inexact form of expression that revealed more of our own artistic intentions than those of whom we imitated. In fact, talking recently to Richard

Robbins, who preceded me by several years at the U of M, he felt confident that Dick took great delight in being imitated, or at least seemed unaware of it when it occurred. But Dick also warned in one of his essays that he was going to teach us to write like him, and our job was to not learn the lesson—a Hugo-like inversion of Whitman's "I am the teacher of athletes, / He that by me spreads a wider breast than my own proves the width of my own, / He most honors my style who learns under it to destroy the teacher." The message from Dick was muddled: Do as I say, and probably not as I do.

Our unlucky fellow student received his comeuppance that day. Dick lowered his glasses, looked over his rims, disgust on his face. He regarded each one of us in the circle gathered around him, and said, to no one in particular: "Why do I have the dirty feeling somebody's got his hand in my pocket?" I remember only being relieved that it was not I who had fucked up so magnificently as to elicit that response. Though I might have wondered why another young man had done with his own private impulse toward language as I had done the year before.

☙☙

By the first day of winter term 1981, I still had not met Richard Hugo. That day, I followed a squat man down the hallway of the English Department. He seemed as wide as he was tall, limping, gasping for air, and sweating despite the January cold that swept up the stairwell from the outside doors a floor below. He turned into Walter King's office and plopped down painfully in a chair. "God, it's good to be back, Walter," he said. It took me a moment, but I realized: This is Hugo. Later, when I introduced myself, I was tongue-tied. I had no idea how to make conversation. The best I could do, there in the hall outside Walter King's office, was, "I'm going to be your student." I think I was looking at my feet. Dick said nothing. No doubt he just grinned and nodded (I would later become familiar with this expression of stunned hilarity that often appeared on his face, and came to believe that it actually meant: How much longer must I endure this?) I would not be his student, however, at least not that winter. Within days he was in Seattle, being treated for lung cancer.

I did not see my ill-starred future teacher again until the following summer, when he gave a charity reading in the basement of a local church, just prior to a showing of *Northern Lights*, a glacially paced, 16mm black and white, independent socialist film about the conspiracy of government and commerce to control or destroy the small Midwestern farmer in the winter of 1915. Dick looked tanned and much thinner, fit, dressed in chinos and Madras shirt. He read from *The Right Madness on Skye*. My wife remembers him not seeming fit at all, but tired, sitting down, and breathing with difficulty. I recall him standing, reciting his poems in a robust voice. Whatever the case, or whatever our different perceptions may suggest, we agree that he seemed gregarious, funny, and relaxed with the nonliterary activist crowd, come to show their solidarity with the local Sanctuary Movement. We saw him again later that summer, at a reading by Maxine Kumin, after which there was a screening of Dave and Annick Smith's short film, *Kicking the Loose Gravel Home*, a tribute to Dick's life and work. Again, I remember a man tanned and vigorous-looking as he stood on stage and received the crowd's applause.

I would take only three courses from my first acknowledged literary mentor—two writing workshops and a techniques of poetry class. The latter was a seminar, the nominal (and improbable) subject of which was Wallace Stevens, about whom, it turned out, Dick had precious little to say, despite their shared interest in the fictional "scene" of a poem. The quality of teaching in each of these classes varied, according to the physical discomfort of our teacher, who, I do not think many of us were quite willing to admit, was dying before our very eyes.

Dick, however, was always early to class. I would be on time, slipping in a few minutes before the hour, but Dick was always there in his seat well before I or anyone else arrived. This was no small matter, I thought, trying to explain to myself why Dick was the only teacher I ever had who arrived before his students. Dick's job began at a particular time. One goes early to work, so as to be ready to begin on time. It was an expression of class: a matter first of having a little class, but also of possessing the working-class expectation about the necessity of one's work, despite any other reservations one might have about the nature or quality of that work. Times were not so good that one could behave in a haughty manner. I grew up, after all, in a household that sent its day labor to the mill at four in the morning, sharp. The shift began at five, and it was a fifteen-minute drive to the factory down the hill. One was always on time, which meant that one would always be early. The message was clear: Never allow the goldbricking wealthy bastard son of the shop's owner to hang your being late over your head! Dick would be sitting in his chair, hunched over, staring at us over the rims of his glasses. His stare was benign before the hour, hostile after. The students who had graduated from state universities tended to be on time, and those who were late seemed oblivious to the glare.

I remember little from the writing workshops, only a handful of comments Dick made about specific poems. He urged us to concentrate on strong rhythms; doing so, our imagination would be liberated from the tyranny of our good intentions. He encouraged us to write lines propelled by loud, pyrotechnical, hard consonants. The semicolon, he warned, was always to be avoided: "For Christ's sake, it's ugly; besides, who really knows how to use it?" He was critical of anyone who repeated the same noun too many times in a poem—"Evidence that the imagination is in park," a comment that echoed his love of big Buicks with automatic transmissions that did not trouble the driver, but delivered him at his destination. Many nights he was lively, frisky even, and hilariously vulgar. Though I recall little of what he said, I see him clearly enough, his glasses now on top of his bald head, sitting upright, one hand over his mouth, the other high in the air, almost bouncing in his seat. "Yasss . . . ?" he asked, awaiting our feeble comments, before he spoke regally about the poems he enjoyed: "By this point in the poem, you can say whatever you god damn well please. I'll believe you even if you say you're waltzing with dolphins in your arms. By God, just keep talking." If he disliked a poem, he would make a face like a man who had just stepped barefoot in a fresh pile of dog shit. Then he would say, with disarming self-consciousness, as though it were his own fault for being so stupid, "I haven't a god damn clue what you're doing here." The offending student felt guilty and promised to try harder.

On bad nights, Dick would take his medication with a six-pack of Bud Tall Boys and would sit there, staring over the rims of his glasses at us, tired, sick, glum, and no doubt weary of our lousy poems, with which he was wasting the last precious hours of his dwindling life. Most of us believed, as many young MFA students do, that each of us alone possessed the next hot ticket to Fame, that our apprentice work was actually the work of genius. We were all of us a bunch of rockin' Rimbauds. And not one of us seemed aware of what Dick already knew: as poets, only a handful of us would survive the lack of attention that would hound us in the years after our insular workshop disbanded and we went our separate and crushingly anonymous ways.

〰

The most memorable course I took from Dick was not a poetry workshop, but his Wallace Stevens seminar. One of his envious junior literature colleagues sniped, "I wouldn't trust him on that subject, any more than I'd trust him on Rilke," a poet Dick apparently had tried and, in this colleague's opinion failed, to teach a few years earlier. I felt defensive, though it is true that Dick seemed ill at ease in an academic setting. And Dick did not have a great deal to say about Stevens. Dick's health, however, played as big a role in his performance as his lack of academic rigor and complete absence of institutional decorum. In class, at noon, he often looked pale and tired, and had difficulty breathing. He limped into the room with the early arrivals, lowered himself into a chair, and at the hour would begin, as often as not, to read from a critical study of "The Comedian as the Letter C." It was just awful—both the incomprehensible academic prose and his mystified reading of it.

Finally, what Dick had to say about Stevens was of little consequence. What he talked about, however, was revealing enough, at least in terms of what it revealed about him and the nature of his own work. The only thing I can remember him actually saying about Stevens was that had he, Dick, written a stanza as rhythmically strong and image-rich as the second stanza of "Two at Norfolk," he would have gone on to set off a battery of fireworks, all the while booming like Vachel Lindsey on the big bass drum. Dick then read the last line of the stanza, as was his practice in his own work, eliding the conjunction and verb of being: "His daughter a foreign thing." But as the poem continues, Dick complained incredulously, "Stevens turns away, abandons the energy of that language." I'm not so sure about this claim, though his comment no doubt reveals more about Dick's lack of subtlety (he, of course, adored Stevens' word "gurrituck") than it does about Stevens, a poet of indisputably greater (and gentler) genius. Stevens ends his poem abruptly, without crescendo or pyrotechnics.

By the time we discussed "Idea of Order," Dick had turned the Stevens class over to any of us who were willing to get up and teach for a day. A few volunteered. I went first, with a lecture on "Farewell to Florida," in which I more or less ignored the craft of the poem. Instead, I followed the easier, time-honored ad hominem approach, criticizing the poet's distress over the fecundity of the Florida Keys. I equated this fecundity, of course, with female sexuality, which at my age I was quite an advocate of, though Stevens insists otherwise. I walked the class line-by-line through the poet's dismissal of a green world I worshiped and that, as Americans, descendants of Roethke, I felt we should all be inclined to embrace. We lived in the American West, after all, wilderness shouldering its way to the very brink of the surrounding foothills. That may have been Stevens' purpose, in part, to resist exactly what I insisted he must open himself toward, but the idea of such contrariety was not something I would have considered then. It was sad, I concluded, to witness a poet who seemed bitterly determined to renounce with hatred such a lushly Romantic landscape. Stevens instead longs to immerse himself in the cold, dark, crowded, and filthy north. That Stevens could write from a variety of linguistic, intellectual, and psychological positions, and thus in his poems developed a lively and complex relationship to the world (the human and non-human) around him—which Roethke later advocated as the poet's primary responsibility—was a fact that eluded me then.

After class, however, Dick said, "Come to my office—now." I followed him down the stairs to the English Department. He sat down with a sigh.

"Jeeesus Christ!" he yelled, as best as he could. "I don't know my ass from a fucking hole in the ground. Why the hell haven't you said something sooner? I thought you were just stupid. God damn it, Ax-el-rod! You think I like listening to myself? For Christ's sake, you're smart, but you never say a god damned thing! How about a little chatter, Ax-el-rod?" I must have seemed mortified because he was laughing by then, shaking all over with delight at my discomfort. He was paying me a compliment.

"Thanks a lot," I muttered and backed out of his office, wondering what in the world to make of such moment. "I'll try to be more help."

During the term Dick taught his Stevens course, he received a copy of the new *Collected Poems* of Bernard Spencer, a poet not

many people read today (my University of Oregon library copy of
Aegean Islands and Other Poems was last checked out in 1962). As
Dick portrayed him, Spencer was a literary ally of the young Auden
and Spender, all of whose work Dick lived and breathed in every
pore of his body. I still recall his flawless, delightful recitations of
Auden's poems (yes, in the Stevens course), especially his regal
and sardonic saying of the poem "Law Like Love." But Spencer
was another matter altogether. Here was something new. Dick
started out just reading a few poems, then looked up at us. "You
hear? I stole everything from this guy!" he confessed, and started
to laugh. "So long as his poems were out of print, everything was
in the god damn bag." Dick wagged his head side to side, looking,
as always, over the rim of his glasses, eyes bright with laughter.
"Jeeesus Christ, now everybody's going to know what a fucking
fraud I am!" He read a poem, "Egyptian Dancer at Shubra," then
recited his own poem, "Dancer at Kozani's." They were uncomfort-
ably similar. An undercurrent of sexual violence runs through each
poem. The men in Dick's poem "whipped her [the dancer] with
our eyes"; Spencer describes "the dancer's sway / hung like a body
to be flogged." Each poem ends with its focus pulling away from
the dancer to the humdrum lives of the unsatisfied men who
watched her. Poets steal, we are taught, they do not parrot. But
Dick was not making that point this time as he went on, revealing
each intersection of Spencer's and his own work, though in fact
the intersection was more subtle than the subjects or contents of
the poems themselves. Spencer had lived in that Mediterranean
landscape Dick had bombed during his service in the Air Force in
World War Two. As a considerable number of his poems
demonstrate, Dick struggled through the middle of his life to
rediscover that landscape, to make peace with himself and the
world he had contributed to the wounding of. Spencer, I think,
was a kind of anodyne for Dick when he was younger; he at least
offered a more intimate, alternative vision of the same landscape,
delivered in a not-too-formal, syntactically odd, and politically

left style Dick adored. "One day in Seattle, over drinks," he confided to us, "I read this stuff to Wagoner and Kizer. And Condor shouted, 'So, that's where you stole your rhythms!' "

Another moment from the Stevens class that had nothing to do with Stevens occurred the day Dick read poems from William Stafford's recently published *Collected Poems*. He sat in front of us, seldom looking up from the book except to comment on a line or image he particularly admired. Nothing about his performance was noteworthy really, until the very end of class. Just before the bell rang, Dick began reciting from memory "Our Town Is Guarded by Automatic Rockets." At the end of the poem—"And I think our story should go on, and not in the dark with nobody listening"—Dick's voice cracked. He was crying, and shook his head from side to side. "What a dear, dear man," he said, "what a dear, dear man." Embarrassed, we filed out and left Dick sitting there, lost in his many griefs.

That William Stafford, and this poem in particular, would evoke such a strong response from Dick revealed more to me than all the classes I had already sat through. Surely, this poem's last line resonated with Dick at that moment, given his awareness of his own mortality. But I felt then, too, that Dick's response to this poem had a great deal to do with his and Stafford's different experiences during the war. Dick, as he wrote, was "willingly confused by the times." Stafford, apparently, was not, and his ethical self-assurance consistently finds expression in such poems as Dick read to us that day. Later, of course, he felt appalled by this self-deception and what it permitted him to participate in, all of which is played out in his poems, where he claimed to be developing a literary persona, "The Leslie Howard of poetry," as he liked to say. Another incarnation was Al "Mush-Heart" Barnes, his private-detective character who shares much of the same sensibility of Dick's poetic persona—always dissembling, apologetic, now a voyeur of destitution, but also a kind of reluctant servant of the poor and disgraced. The older man, Stafford, in response to the various threats and seductions of power in confusing times, was so self-confident (read *Down in My Heart*) he could resist, take a difficult but clear and consistent ethical stance.

Dick earned for himself a more conflicted fate than Stafford's. The contrition, alienation, self-debasement, and melancholy that run throughout Dick's poems, and that are the source of much of his most powerful work, were, nevertheless, the stance of a younger man, a stance Dick had long outgrown by the time I encountered his writing and then came to sit at his feet. Stafford, given his prolixity of subjects and experiences, written from a stance of bright psychic health and robustness, offered Dick a lighted path toward maturity and reconciliation that he had stumbled upon only in a handful of his last and perhaps best poems—"Sea Lanes Out," "Here, But Unable to Answer," "Making Certain It Goes On," "Distances," poems that began to break the rhetorical patterns that had trapped him for over a decade, poems that still shake us with their unusual candor.

♫♫

Whatever Dick's intentions that day in his office when he upbraided me for not saving him sooner from the humiliation of teaching Stevens, afterwards he treated me far more warmly than I had ever expected. I still did not talk a lot in class, but I did say hello without blushing, and invited Dick to dance parties, where he sat in a stuffed chair, watching us whirl around the room at 2 a.m., Hound Dog Taylor, Big Joe Turner, Alberta Hunter, and Eddie Cleanhead Vinson blaring from the hi-fi. He kept shouting and laughing, in his propulsive, alliterative English: "God damned good tunes guys!" Soon, his wife, Ripley, appeared to lead him home to Wiley Street— a street name his editors would not allow him to adopt as his nom de plume for the mystery *Death and the Good Life*.

After graduation I even had the nerve (actually Walter Pavlich had to coax me to make the call) to invite Dick and Ripley to my wedding reception, which was down the Bitterroot Valley south of Missoula, at the Bass Creek picnic area. We planned to drink a keg of beer, eat BBQ, and play volleyball until dark, which in Montana in summer is always late in arriving. Road construction backed up traffic for miles on one of the hottest days of the year. Dick showed up nevertheless, alone, tanned, and in good spirits. I introduced him to my relatives, one of whom, my grandmother, said, "You've done a great job with our Davy," believing I suppose that Dick was somehow responsible for my marrying a member of the human race.

When he felt well and his mood was jovial, as it was that day, Dick did not miss the opportunity a straight line offered. He vigorously pumped my grandmother's hand and said, "And I just want to say what a fine job you all did with this young man, considering what lousy material you had to work with."

My family, not noted for its sense of humor, all covered their mouths in one motion and laughed at this, scandalized, though it confirmed, I suppose, what they had thought all along since I moved to Montana.

The reception was a success. We drank the keg, ate our fill of chicken, green salad, baked beans, and cake, and played volleyball, as Dick held forth to a small crowd at a picnic table. Josefa and I left at dusk, not long after Dick met my mother (then in the throes of early middle age). "One hot broad, Axelrod," he said to me aside and beaming. I had never heard anyone speak quite that way about my mother before, though it was the sort of thing one might expect Dick to say—yes, a compliment, spoken with great sincerity and admiration for its object.

Driving home, we followed the frontage road along U.S. 93. The horned moon hung at the crest of the Bitterroots. As we came over a rise, an oncoming car entered our lane. I swerved hard onto the shoulder and into the grass, then swerved back onto the road, almost tipping over our little car with its bald tires, and cursing the fool who had nearly killed us, but certain from that point, too, of our good luck. Dick would not be so lucky. Within two months, he was back in Seattle, ill with cancer. By October, he was dead.

❧❧

Already that fall, even as I looked forward to Dick's recovery and fishing with him as he had promised, "up the Blackfoot," at Upsata Lake, I was beginning to question the local party line about his poetry, a doubt Dick had planted about himself and his work. He had warned us repeatedly against "the mask becoming the man." This, he felt, had happened to him, at least at one point earlier in his career. That mask is the subject of his poem "Second Chances," a poem that shook me deeply for many years:

> I can't let it go, the picture I keep of myself
> in ruin, living alone, some wretched town
> where friendship is based on just being around.
> And I drink there a lot, stare at the walls until
> the buzzing of flies becomes the silence I drown in.

In the middle of the poem, he turns for a stanza to discussing his present circumstances—happily married, a literary and financial success—concluding, "Three years ago, I wouldn't / have given a dime for my chances in life." There is a tone of pleading about this stanza. And so I hear a rumor of the disingenuous here, as though the poet cannot quite remove the mask he has worn so long. And the last stanza suggests very loudly that the speaker fears that he cannot shake the mask he once wore, and because of this, the domestic love he values now is as vulnerable to loss as ever:

> [A] vagabond knocks at the door. I go answer
> and he says, "Come back, baby. You'll find
> a million poems deep in your destitute soul."

And I say, "Go away, Don't ever come back."
But I watch him walk, always downhill toward
the schoolyard where children are playing 'ghost,'
a game where, according to the rules, you take
another child's name in your mind but pretend
you're still you while others guess your new name.

It is a sad-sounding prospect. Trying to be someone else while seeming to be yourself, and those from your past, who recognize you, know it is just a game, and are laughing. There is little to be hopeful about. Rhetorically, too, the poem develops no differently than any of Dick's work: narrative exposition, evaluation, re-evaluation, the trajectory of which is a deeply felt truth about the "destitute" self, and so it echoes the patterns that make up the bulk of Dick's poetry in the 1970s. But also, the poem at least suggests Dick's awareness of the problem. The shame is that he did not live long enough to find his way out of this aesthetic and personal dilemma.

My doubts began at the reading I heard Dick deliver in the spring of 1982, and though I was spellbound by his performance, it left me with an uneasy feeling. Dick did not read, he recited. And his recitation, for all its bardic quality, was nevertheless a calculated bit of acting. His jokes, though good (we laughed), were anything but spontaneous. At the beginning of the reading, he opened a thermos. His hands trembled as he poured a clear liquid into his cup. "It's water," he said. "I used to drink vodka from this thermos during a reading, but it made my hands shake." As he said this, his trembling hand spilled water all over the counter. He was immediately sympathetic, in a comic way, not unlike many of Woody Allen's early schlemiel characters. He paced back and forth, limping as he recited his best-known work from the sixties and seventies. It was wonderful, the way any Greatest Hits album is wonderful, at least the first time you listen to it, delighted by recognition and confirmation. What made me uneasy were the introductions to the poems. One, the introduction to "Plans for Altering the River," was comic. He told the "true story behind this poem," in which a large landowner is given the Key to the City of Seattle for agreeing to sell his land for a proposed expansion of SeaTac airport. By the time he began his poem, without any pause or transition, "All those in favor of our plans to alter the river, / please raise your hands," many of us were so involved in the story we began to raise our hands! I snatched my hand back, but looked around at the many people in the crowd who had been tricked into voting against the sentiments of the poem.

The introduction to "What Thou Lovest Well Remains American" was even more problematic. Because I was more familiar with this poem, I was not going to be suckered. I began to wonder what Dick was up to as he retold the story of the Grubskis in such a way as to draw a kind of nervous but condescending laughter from the audience. I knew, and a few others I glanced at knew the same thing, too, that what approached was anything but funny. I recall looking at a good friend and former student of Dick's, Paul Zarzyski, who sat without apparent emotion as Dick regaled the audience with the many humiliations of the Grubskis, a creepy family of freaks beyond all hope for redemption. The audience split its side, more or less, until Dick began reciting the poem. The result was to humiliate the audience for its cruelty toward those least able to defend themselves, and with whom Dick identifies at the end of the poem. His humor was curiously spiteful, and used finally to direct our mean-spiritedness at himself.

♌ ♌

As apprentice writers, we may run afoul of The Law and stupidly parrot others. Worse, though, as mature writers, we may end up parroting only ourselves. Milosz writes that "The purpose of poetry is to remind us / how difficult it is to remain just one person." Somehow, and I am not certain I know exactly how, we must resist ourselves and especially those who would admire us and our work, and in doing so keep the ego from blocking the open doorway to the world that is always inviting us to life beyond the boundaries of the self. Much of Dick Hugo's poetry is a sad demonstration of this fact, for which we, as his students and audience, are perhaps in part to blame. I do not want to engage in any kind of psycho-biography in regard to Dick, so suffice it to say that his insistence that a poet must always establish a *modus operandi,* and "stabilize the basis of operations" betrayed his deep apprehensions about letting go of the mask he wore in his poems. The mask, however, is one of the cultural privileges of living in the American West, where self-creation is the primary occupation of newcomers and long-time residents alike, and often results in their assuming one of the few mythic personae available.

Besides its strong emotions, there was so little else for a young writer like myself in the early 1980s to learn from Dick Hugo's poetry, other than how easy it was to imitate his overpowering voice, "over-stance," and virile style. Our responsibility as students was always to reject Dick's teaching. But so few of us were willing to do that, and instead we spent hours in bars devising elaborate degradations so that we, too, might assume an "authentic" voice like our mentor's. It was absurd. Many of us just quit writing in humiliation. Others changed genres. But not once did I ever hear anyone wonder why this was happening. At the public tribute after his death, homage was paid again and again to the hard-drinking, hard-living, but always tender-hearted and doomed man; those who eulogized him honored the mask he had worn in his poems, that I suppose I have honored here, too, that had become confused with the actual man, and that he wished, by the end, he could have removed. Perhaps then he may have realized the potential greatness that had so long been stifled in his work.

Dick Hugo was an unlikely mentor, though others I know valued his mentorship in ways far more conventional and constructive than I. If they have not already, in time I hope that they will all tell stories. Whatever I learned from Dick was, for the most part, by negative example. Powerful as many of his poems are (and how many of us who were his students have written or ever will write anything approaching the power of his best poems?), whenever I read them now, I am always left with an uneasy feeling of having witnessed a man hurrying himself toward an artistic dead end. The limited occasion for poetry that Dick defined as a "triggering town," by his middle age rendered his work a self-parody that he struggled to outgrow, and only did, perhaps, in a few poems the last difficult year of his life. Or perhaps Dick's instincts were correct: to locate meaning not in the pretty postcard scenery of majestic wilderness, but in the predicament of our history in this place, the wounds we inflicted on both the landscape and its people. But throughout his most productive years, Dick ignored the advice of his own mentor, Theodore Roethke, who believed a poet should write a variety of poems that reflect the diverse ways in which the psyche interacts with the world—the meditation, the ornate lyric, the joke, the ode, the epigram, and so on. Dick's mentorship for me became a caution about the dangers of defining a poem (and by extension, one's self and life) too narrowly in its occasion, its tone, and stance. By the time I arrived in his classes, Dick had long mined the vein of his own early deep feeling to exhaustion, was sometimes parroting himself, and sometimes despising those foolish students who demonstrated how easy it was to assume the mask he wore in his own poems. And there was the first lesson I learned about the psychic space of the Western American landscape into which I had been drawn by Dick's voice: so long as I remained naïve, it could kill me, too.

A Habit of Mind

I worked a strange shift that year—one p.m. to ten p.m.—and so, between the months of August and May, the brief period when we lived in the house on the cliff above the Big Blackfoot River, I climbed home in the dark along the cliff trail. Two hundred and sixty-five nights. The majority of those nights during what seemed to us then, uninitiated as we were, the most severe winter of our lives.

From the moment we first climbed it, the cliff trail meant a great deal more to me than I could clearly understand or articulate. That trail, and my nightly encounters with its switchbacks, insisted that I not mistake my own perception, as young men often will, as the universal perception of reality. "That trail" was actually many trails, or the habits of many minds and their different ways of knowing the particular place.

Like Rilke's archaic torso of Apollo, that trail was appraising me, demanding a change in my life. When I left the house on the mountain at noon each weekday, Josefa and our infant son waved goodbye and turned back ambivalently to their solitude on the verge of the cliff. Returning at night and seeing the lights of our house as I crossed the ridge and dogs came to greet me at Windy Boy Point, I felt no such ambivalence. Though perhaps I suspected even then that Josefa, standing in the window, hoping to catch sight of me, calculated other possibilities concerning the figure who approached along the trail.

There were options for making my way home other than climbing the cliff to our house. I could drive home, until Thanksgiving, when snow closed the logging road that wound into Wild Mint Gulch and past the rutted quarter-mile-long two-track we called, improbably, "our driveway." But to drive up the mountain meant driving on the highway several more miles up the Big Blackfoot canyon past our house, crossing the river at Wisherd Landing, unlocking the gate, turning down the abandoned railroad bed, and then returning three miles on the north side of the river, before even beginning the ascent to our house. Having retraced the three miles back down the canyon, the road up Wild Mint Gulch turned off from the railbed and climbed steeply for several more miles before achieving the ridge above our house. It was quicker to walk.

I chose to climb home along the cliff trail because it was quicker, and because it was open to starlight and moonlight sufficient to illuminate the path at my feet. Older friends of ours had built the trail before the logging company punched the road into the forests on Wisherd Ridge to clear-cut, as a chip-truck driver explained to us one day, "for hog fuel"—old growth reduced to chips to fire the boiler at the plywood plant. Our friends had lived with their young children in a small cottage along the river below the cliff. They saved their money to buy the cliff and the twenty-five acres behind it so that they could build their dream home—a contemporary tri-level suburban box. They purchased a kit for the house and carried it—first on their backs and then, when they could afford them, on mules—piece by piece up the trail they constructed. The madness of this endeavor is of a magnitude that can only be understood if one considers their youth and relative poverty at that time. They were going to have a new house, even if they had to carry it up a cliff.

There were eight switchbacks along the cliff. The trail began where a path led from the footbridge through alders to the north side of the railbed and a weathered hand-painted sign, "Private Trail." With the exception of two tree-sheltered wide places, the path was no more than one foot wide. The trail climbed first across a talus slope, switchbacked at a dead ponderosa, backtracked across the top of the talus, then switchbacked again into more stable rock ledges that ascended through sparse trees to The Washout, about halfway up the trail. The Washout was a gap in the trail, where our friends had attempted to construct it on a bare rock face. They succeeded initially, building up a rock wall, back-filling with gravel, and topping it with a firm layer of packed dirt. But eventually it eroded, then collapsed, was repaired, eroded and collapsed again, and then left unrepaired. To cross The Washout, I needed to step high with my right foot onto the single foothold, and then lead with my left foot across the four-foot gap, pushing off with the right foot to propel myself through the open space. To fall here might not have been fatal. If I had fallen, I would have tumbled twenty feet, but might have rolled a considerable distance further, if the trunk of a ponderosa did not break the fall. But I could have rolled and slid the entire four hundred feet to the railbed, by which point I would have been very dead.

Not far above The Washout, near the fifth switchback, was Rocky Boy Point, the widest place on the cliff, with a broad rock outcropping on which to sit and look up or down the Big Blackfoot canyon. Above this, the trail switchbacked quickly through two steep turns, then one long switchback before reaching the ridge at Windy Boy Point, where it leveled out as it approached the house.

ℒℒ

The trail presented Josefa and me with a dilemma that was obvious the first time we climbed it together. The isolation of the house on the mountain represented our two vastly different perceptions of what our experiences there would consist of. The feeling of being at some considerable remove from the highway, the conduit to society, filled me with an Adamic wonder. That such a feeling was a delusion remained far from my mind then; I believed in the purifying solitude that lay ahead of (or above) us. The entire landscape was ours alone to discover, explore, and name. For Josefa, a new mother, still suffering from post-partum depression, and with only a few women friends to confide in, the house on the mountain came to be a cruel episode of exile in the midst of natural beauty. Her isolation pushed her to the border of madness, as the house itself bordered on the verge of a cliff. For me, the cliff kept an unwanted world at a distance, so that I could pretend to inhabit an infinitely lovely and harsh kingdom of my own. I know now what she must have feared then about that cliff: how near we permitted ourselves to come to disaster. I told her how fortunate she was to live in the presence of what I perceived, with no more depth of understanding than what one might casually call "nice scenery," as beautiful and wild.

Our friends, the original owners of the house on the mountain, and from whom we had been renting a small cabin ten miles farther up the Blackfoot, were looking for someone to live in their former dream home. Their son, daughter-in-law, and two grandchildren—the marriage dissolving—had just moved out, and our friends were concerned about leaving the house vacant.

So, without a thought about the influence life on that cliff had on the previous occupants, we agreed to take a look.

We parked, crossed the footbridge and began ascending the trail, me in the lead, with our infant son on my back. All I recall about that first ascent along the trail was crossing The Washout ("We could get used to this"), stopping at Rocky Boy Point, and my turning to Josefa to say something to the effect that the trail was gloriously difficult, a hardship, an ordeal to master. She was not convinced. Far more clearly than any sophistry of mine was the furrow in her brow. She stood below me, the cliff side so steep we could not actually see the entire slope, only the open space between us and the river. She was horrified at the extremes to which her husband seemed willing to go. She told me I was out of my god damn mind. And we laughed.

When we arrived at the house that first time, however, it seemed palatial in comparison to our one-room cabin: spacious, bright rooms with high ceilings, hardwood floors, massive stone fireplaces, windows that framed the Sapphire Mountains and Big Blackfoot canyon. It was an easy pleasure to imagine our domestic life within that fine house. She liked it. And as I was determined to have an adventure, she permitted it, in spite of her doubts. The "fine scenery"—a geography framed by picture windows and rendered merely pretty—also conspired against us as we stood at the glass where we would soon sit down to share our meals. A late-afternoon thunderstorm passed over the mountains and swept up the canyon. As the sun reappeared in its wake, a rainbow formed. What was peculiar about that rainbow was the perspective from which we observed it. We stood at a sharp angle above the rainbow, looking down through the arch. A lordly perspective.

❦

We moved to the mountain during the year of our president's "Evil Empire" speech, and spent that time cutting twenty cords of firewood, trying to prepare ourselves for the first snow or the nuclear oblivion his ideological brinkmanship promised. We celebrated our first wedding anniversary in August. The Indian Summer that followed was glorious, and as we lay in the forest with our son, resting in the warm afternoon light, the smell of sawdust on our clothes, we allowed ourselves the luxury of believing such days might go on without end.

The road off the mountain was still open, and my family often met me in town for dinner, to visit friends, or run errands during my long afternoon break after the newspaper went to press. In the mornings and on weekends, when we were not cutting or hauling firewood, we walked the mountain from river to ridge, giving all its features names: Fairway of the Bears, Beaver Bend, Bear Island, Hidden Valley, Eagle Tower, Half Moon Meadow, October Park,

Lost Horse Meadow, and on the high point of Wisherd Ridge: Nine-Geese-Cross-the-Sun. Each name evoked a specific story or characteristic of a place that existed on a new kind of map, not two-dimensional, rather a linguistic map that integrated into the landscape our personal lives and the presence of those living in proximity to us, with whom we shared the trails. This was precisely the Adamic adventure I intended.

The third week of November, we were still possessed by an unfamiliar and joyful expansiveness. We planned a big Thanksgiving feast, inviting our friends and former teachers from Missoula to join us in our exotic aerie on the mountain. It would be a jolly time. The weather remained warm and dry for late November, and so we were confident about transporting even the oldest guests up the mountain without jeopardy. Josefa met them at the footbridge and chauffeured them up the logging road. The others followed, walking in the dark with me along the road to avoid the hazards of the cliff trail. We ate and drank and talked for hours, until someone suggested that we go outside to look at the stars.

It was snowing. The ground was already covered by six inches of snow, fallen in just the few hours we sat blindly inside. Drunk as we were, everyone decided to clean up, then walk down the mountain together to the cars. In the meantime, I wrestled our two vehicles down to the highway, parking each and climbing the trail twice in the time it took to clean up. Then the happy, drunken party stepped out into the night and made its way singing and laughing back down the road to the cars, where our friends waved goodbye and we turned back toward the mountain that had vanished in the snowy dark.

♊

Just so, we passed into early winter on the mountain. It was still snowing Monday when I went to work, and continued to snow until four feet lay around the house. When it cleared later in the week, the temperature fell to thirty below zero and remained there until Christmas, rising only to near zero whenever it would snow again. And snow it did. Every few days another several inches would fall. Because of our position on the west side of Sheep Mountain and Wisherd Ridge, the storms piled up directly above us and dropped the greater portion of their moisture on our house. By the time Chinook winds came up the valley from the south in late January, there was more than five feet of hard-packed snow.

Thanksgiving morning, hours before the arrival of the party, a friend had delivered a wood stove that he sold to us for thirty-five dollars (installed), aware that even with our twenty cords of Douglas fir we could not heat the house through December if we continued to use the fireplaces. Our daily routine began with waking early to stoke the fires, splitting firewood and kindling, and carrying in a day's (and night's) supply to the woodstove in the basement and to the fireplace upstairs. These chores finished, we wrote at our desks while Yascha napped on the floor beside us, then we snowshoed or skied around the mountain until late morning, at which time I prepared to leave for work.

I was not consciously aware of what Josefa faced alone on the mountain. I kissed her and Yascha goodbye, hurried down the trail to the footbridge, crossed the river, and drove away in the one car that still started despite the cold. Her experience of the next ten hours was vastly different than mine. I used to say I envied her being able to remain on the mountain alone with our son. I would gladly trade places, I told her, only to know the mountain intimately throughout the afternoon and evening. To this she never responded.

Once the deepest cold settled into the canyon, the cheap battery in our one functioning car no longer charged. The morning I discovered this, I had to hitchhike, which brought me home to climb the trail (rides east out of Missoula being few) not until after midnight. So I carried the battery up and down the mountain each day and night in order to assure that the car would start and I would be able to go to work.

It was at this time, too, that the sun slipped behind Bonner Mountain, directly south of us, and plunged the house into a perpetual daytime twilight. I could leave each day and drive into Missoula, where it may or may not have been sunny, but where, at least, on sunny days I could spend a moment in full light. My family never enjoyed this privilege, remaining behind on the mountain week after week. On weekends, of course, I was reluctant to leave the mountain, the very place I wished to remain, and so my family had to content itself with the company of the New Adam, who, climbing the trail one night, saw a herd of elk cross the river ice near the mouth of Johnson Creek. Delighted by having witnessed something so rare in his life, he named that spot Ice Crossing. At home that night, he penciled the name on a topographic map that hung by thumb tacks to the wall.

ℒℒ

We were not always alone on the mountain after the snow began to fall. There were a few vigorous people we were confident we could invite to climb the cliff trail for visits. Others, such as an uninvited visitor in late winter, could be problematic. The uninvited visitor refused to walk anywhere on or off the mountain, and had to be dragged to the highway on a toboggan, and soon vanished from our lives. One friend climbed the trail more often than any other and was witness to the single most treacherous moment on the trail. One night, as I led him down the trail, I slipped on a particularly steep, exposed portion. I was not frightened or even particularly flustered, landing on my ass, legs dangling off the ledge. He looked at me in silence for a long moment, considering the situation as any bachelor rancher from Brown County, Nebraska, might. "You ought not to do that too often," he drawled.

At Christmas, we arranged with several friends to exchange gifts and enjoy a feast of the sort the four of us could afford. It snowed on Christmas Eve. I was at work, and during my break, bought groceries for Christmas dinner, which I carefully packed into my backpack. My supervisor sent me home early to climb the trail, in the dark nevertheless, in a driving wind and heavy snow, in which I imagined myself, as I stopped to rest against a tree, a man far from any connection to human intimacy except for the trail he climbed.

That night, I was aware for the first time of how the trail represented conflicting tendencies in my own thinking. It permitted me the delusion of living at an ambiguous distance from people, to play briefly each day and night at having an adventure. The trail connected me, nevertheless, to a human form, the thinking that shaped it years before I ever stepped upon it. At either end of the trail, people anticipated my daily coming and going: below, in the parking lot at the Blackfoot Tavern, where the owners craned their necks and shook their heads at my passing; and above, where it ended on the eighth switchback at Windy Boy Point, when I could see the lights of our house despite the windblown snow.

Christmas Day we exchanged gifts with our intrepid friends from town, feasted on goose and wild rice, and skied far up the mountain toward Lost Horse Meadow and October Park, each drifted deep in new snow. The day had cleared, and the fresh snow still clung to all the trees on the mountains. Bonner Mountain across the canyon to the south loomed up closer in the clear, cold air, the forests on its northern flank blue-white and pristine, and seemingly alive with a deep-toned thrum. And although the day began cold, the radio reporting that Elk Park near Butte set a record with minus sixty-four degrees, the temperature began to moderate, rising to two degrees above zero. This was cause for celebration. We drank a bottle of Irish Mist in late afternoon, toasted the good fortune of warmer days. But as always, I soon walked our friends down the trail in the dark, waved goodbye at the bridge, and returned along the cliff face to our snowbound house.

~~

After Christmas, the temperatures moderated again, briefly, then an ice storm stranded us. We could look over the cliff edge at the highway, where the customary sound of traffic had fallen silent. We waited a long week for ice to thaw. By the new moon, the temperature rose again, briefly, then fell, snow followed, and our lives resumed their ordinary routine.

The night of the full moon in January was our crisis. I spent that night in a frenzy after returning home along the trail. I do not recall the precise circumstances, but soon after my return, we quarreled and I stormed out of the house, wandering all night along animal trails higher up the mountain, imagining myself transformed into what, perversely, I considered my ultimate achievement on the mountain: a wild creature. I suspect that I was responding more to Josefa's predicament than I knew or could then understand. Faced with her complaints of boredom, loneliness, and worthlessness, I wished to demonstrate the actual value of the life we chose on that mountain. I suppose that she knew full well the actual value of the so-called "wild self," and left alone with it for long periods of time, also learned to fear it and to know its destructive character. Unable or unwilling to understand that myself, I piously stomped around the mountain all night in blinding moonlight, a werewolf.

But my ungovernable character, my increasingly violent emotions, my reluctance to learn, are typical enough of young men, and typical of the variety of violence that accompanies us into the landscape, where these emotions are not only given a stage on which to perform, but are even, in the American West anyway, mythologized. In my reading at that time, I happened upon a form of ironic anodyne to my excess. The passage seems far more apt to me today, describing the way I behaved that winter, imagining myself separate from social constraints, than it did at the time, when I dismissed it as the jealousy of older men who had lost their youth. Aristotle had this to say about young men like myself:

> *Young men have strong passions, and tend to gratify them indiscriminately. . . . They are changeable and fickle in their desires, which are violent while they last, but quickly over: their impulses are keen but not deep-rooted, and are like sick people's attacks of hunger and thirst. They are hot-tempered, and quick-tempered, and apt to give way to their anger; bad temper often gets the better of them, for owing to their love of honor they cannot bear being slighted, and are indignant if they imagine themselves unfairly treated.*

I dismissed this of course, though surely this was how I felt having to work through daylight hours of the week, and unable, therefore, to enjoy the mountain where I longed to be, and where Josefa had what seemed to me the unjust privilege of being present all day, every day. Why did she fail to feel exalted? Why did she seem ungrateful?

Aristotle then goes on to say that young men "have exalted notions,"

> *because they have not yet been humbled by life or learnt its necessary limitations; moreover, their hopeful disposition makes them think themselves equal to great things—and that means having exalted notions. They would always rather do noble deeds than useful ones . . . all their mistakes are in the direction of doing things excessively and vehemently . . . they think they know everything, and are always quite sure about it; this, in fact, is why they overdo everything.*

I was blind and deaf to how the trail I followed up that cliff was instructing me on the necessity of following a different trail, the one the mind constructs for another but no less crucial way of moving—more gently, ritually, thoughtfully—from one place to another. Clearly, the trail I had made a part of my daily routine was not meant to occupy that central and mock-heroic position in my life, nor should it have been forced upon others. The barrier the trail erected between myself and others less inclined to climb it was no proper measure of the quality or importance of those people's lives. The arrangement of our day-to-day existence smacked of what I am aware now are enormous clichés about masculinity, and about living in the American West: a rugged individual surviving bravely in a hostile but beautiful environment (though living in gaudy suburban luxury a short distance from a major highway), trying to make the land somehow useful to his sublime purposes. The shame and absurdity of it, like a gaping hole in my head, became too much to ignore. If I placed any value at all upon my relations to my family, I would have to quit living my fantasy on the cliff trail.

❧❧

By late January, Chinook winds arrived and winter broke. By February fifth the sun had returned, crossing the ridge-line above us for several hours a day. The cliff face, wherever the sun touched it, however briefly, flowered with sagebrush buttercups. Soon, the trail was free of snow and one Friday night I plowed through the remaining drifts of snow in Wild Mint Gulch, and drove to the house, to the cheers of my family, who came out to witness what seemed like an excellent reason to celebrate. The next morning, we drove off the mountain to Seeley Lake for pie at the Elkhorn Café, the sober weight of the long cold and dark suddenly behind us. Now before leaving for work I climbed the trail many times a day, running down for the newspaper, again for the mail, or went for long walks on Marco Flats along the river with our son while Josefa wrote at her desk. One Sunday evening, two friends came to visit for the first time since fall, and as they stumbled along, following my lead down the mountain in the dark that night, one of them commented, not altogether charitably, as he picked his way awkwardly through the rocks, that I had eyes in my feet. And it was true, I had learned to see in the dark.

We decided in April that we had enough. Certainly Josefa had endured enough beauty and courageous individualism to suit her for a lifetime. The winter had been so difficult for her, we decided to leave Montana, as soon as that opportunity arose. It would be several more years before that opportunity appeared at last, but more importantly, we vowed to work together, sharing equally the responsibilities for the care of our son as well as sharing financial responsibilities—a pact we have kept to this day, twenty years later.

ℒℒ

Twenty years, and still that brief, early moment in our marriage haunts me. There was no rainbow hanging in the air below us as we prepared to move off the mountain—to return first to the cabin where we had lived earlier, farther up the Big Blackfoot River. Then to a farmhouse, where our second son would be born. And later yet, at the end of another summer, we would move to Oregon. Each of these moves would prove to be another violence on our psyches, but necessary as they were difficult. The ambivalences of these decisions we made were many. We left the house on the mountain at just the time our lives there were improving, becoming tolerable again, which was a seduction that might have convinced us to remain. And we moved back to the cabin at just the time the forests and fields that surrounded it were the most lush. We replanted our garden and slipped back into a very comfortable, familiar pattern.

The night we finished packing up to leave the mountain, May Day, it began to snow, and deer gathered at the natural salt lick under the mercury light near the garage. That is the last night-time image I have of the house on the mountain, hiking home along the trail in the snow again, cresting the ridge, and seeing there before me strange shapes of creatures huddled together in a pale halo of light.

Sonata of the Dwindling Year

I n a hurry before the autumn rains began, Nye Escue finished plowing the stubble and seeded his field to winter wheat. That night he fell asleep in his armchair and never woke. Family and friends eulogized him in a downpour, and as they followed his body along the muddy lane to the cemetery, an emerald mist already lay over his field. The wheat deepened in the Indian summer after storms cleared. Then frost drifted out of the mountains to cover the valley with hoar. His wheat field was thriving even as the solstice approached, and a comet, absent from the sky three generations—a pale and formless light—had appeared again in the southeast.

Most nights that autumn when the sky was clear, Darwin, who lived at the crest of the next hill, drove over to my place. We would cross a barbed-wire fence and stand in a weedy pasture, hoping to find the comet both our grandfathers remembered being wakened from their beds as children and taken outside in pajamas to see— a long-haired star arcing across the entire sky. "I saw it for sure," Darwin told me one night as he jerked his truck to a stop in the gravel drive. But he was no stargazer, and what he had actually seen was dusky red Arcturus, setting on the horizon of the southern sky. Another night he pointed higher to Altair, and the next night higher yet at Jupiter, and next he pointed to the southeast at Sirius, shifting colors as it rose on the heels of Orion. That what he saw was not what he thought he saw made little difference. I never corrected him and besides, he was determined to know that beautiful object his grandfather had praised. He claimed his part in that story like a birthright.

But along our road there were others, less hopeful than Nye Escue or Darwin. In late summer, a haze hanging in the air as the mountains turned tinder dry and weeds caught fire in ditches, the old people began warning us how tired they were of appreciating this gift of life. We would listen to them retell their stories and it seemed that they were pleading with us to remember them in an idealized past, a time before poverty or bodily disgrace, before greed robbed those hills of timber and ore and native grass, and violence began carrying away children. And when frost smeared mountains and canyons yellow and orange and scarlet, already the damp cold had infected the bones of those too old to warm themselves in a daily round of chores. Even on warm southerly days when hornets growled inside over-ripe plums, a blue plume of smoke rose from old people's stoves.

One ninety-two-year-old man, living in a single room of his dilapidated house, who had saved all his extra money for the entire year, ordered ten cords of wood from Ray, the woodcutter. All day, each day throughout the coming winter, Ray told me, the old man would sit in a chair, and with a hammer and wedge, split exactly five billets of wood to heat his room. "I'll probably die this winter," he told Ray, "but unless you hear otherwise, deliver me another ten cords next fall."

Others began to glean neighbors' gardens and fields. One family arrived in our driveway, built a fire in the gravel, and canned vats of tomatoes from our garden. Darwin brought another family to gather burlap sacks full of corn I had planned to gather as feed for goats and rabbits. Instead, they sat together silently all afternoon under yellow larches, stripping kernels from cobs of dry corn to grind for meal. Another afternoon late in October, Darwin drove up to our place followed by three truckloads of families and continued on up the hill to the orchard to pick apples I had left high in the trees for the starlings. Their children clung like monkeys in the crowns of the unpruned Winter Banana and Wolf River, shaking down bruised, over-ripe fruit for cider and sauce.

Soon, nothing stood between us and the wind. Many of our neighbors' homes, old trailers or remodeled outbuildings, were like sieves through which the wind poured. With every gust, the carpet along the western wall of our living room billowed up like a sheet pinned down at the corners. Loose patches of linoleum slapped near the kitchen door. Windows rattled. The wet cellar floor froze over and frost crept up the stone foundation. Hanging in bare rafters under our house, a rattlesnake's abandoned skin slowly shredded and scattered its transparent silver scales. The land stiffened and sealed tight, its life retreated as deeply into earth as snakes descend, coiled and warm near a source no one can conjure alive.

There were others, too, who possessed nothing to place between themselves and the changing season. One boy and his pregnant girlfriend took up back into the hills. They had stolen a car, robbed a store in a nearby town, and were hiding out. We learned about them one day in August when the boy's mother began leaving sacks of groceries in weeds alongside the forest road. Josefa's friend, Diana, lived just across the creek bottom in the canyon from there and could see what was happening, though neither she nor any of us thought it especially important to call the sheriff. We left them alone and were happy or busy enough with our own rounds of daily work to forget about those two. But when the alder and willow leaves fell, their trail appeared for all to see, leading from the road back along the margin of the stream, and up into overhanging rocks at the head of the canyon. The story is that the sheriff's deputy stopped to piss, and, seeing a sack of groceries and the trail, figured he knew who was back there. When he and the sheriff found them sitting around a small cook-fire, the girl was no longer pregnant. The baby had died in the cold after its birth in October and they had buried it in soft ground near the creek.

♌♌

And then, three weeks before Christmas, Darwin's son-in-law, Perry, committed suicide. At dusk one evening, cars and trucks began roaring up and down the road, turning in at Darwin's or going on along the ridge to stop at Perry's house. Josefa called from Diana's house down in the canyon. They had just come back from a walk and found a note on the kitchen table. Perry had killed himself, she said, at his parents' ranch. Later, Diana would have an earful of angry gossip about what actually happened and why, but all we knew then was what we learned from Darwin.

He arrived after breakfast the next morning, jerked his red pickup to a stop below the porch, lit a cigarette, and waited until I appeared on the steps. Frost still lay thick on the grass and crunched like spun glass under my boots. Darwin rolled down his window. "I suppose you heard about Perry." I nodded and asked about Darwin's daughter, Cheryl, and his two granddaughters, Twyla and Patty. He shook his head and we went into the cellar under the porch to smoke. It did not occur to me until later what was at stake or how Darwin was providing a necessary cover story to excuse a daughter who had long before strayed from her troubled husband. He of course deliberately wanted to tell Cheryl's side of the story. In Darwin's version of events, Cheryl never appeared as a character much less a provocateur; what he told was Perry's story alone, the story of a man whom he portrayed as nothing less than a victim of the horrors of the century. In spite of what I learned Darwin had left out, and maybe even because of it, it was clear how the trail Perry followed, like that unfortunate girl and her infant in the canyon, never forked from a certain doom.

Perry, I learned, was an illegitimate child born in Germany during the chaos just following the Second World War. His adoptive parents went to Berlin seven years after the surrender, looking for orphaned children: his adoptive father was an American soldier who had been among those liberating the camps and, overcome by the horror he witnessed, returned for the children's sake; and his adoptive mother, though not Jewish, had been a prisoner in a work camp, where she miscarried. From an alchemy of many griefs—from war, Holocaust, defeat, occupation, from the longing of this sterile ranch couple from the American West whose bodies refused to give them the child they desired—appeared the strange alloy of Perry's life.

Brought to America, by age ten he had hanged himself twice from rafters in their barn. By twelve he had tried drowning in the stock pond. Then a long, improbable calm lasting through high school, marriage, the birth of his red-haired, freckled daughters.

All I knew about Perry before he died was that he kept bloodhounds and fussed over a restored roadster, painted an orange brighter than his own bright orange hair. The roadster was his greatest pride, though he never drove it, except to die. For everyday use, he drove an old Chevy pickup. But always, parked there in his drive—its chrome pipes, mag wheels, grill, and roll bar reflecting the intense orange of its buffed metal-flake finish— sat his gleaming metaphor. As for his hounds, they were the most forlorn creatures on our road. Caged in a narrow run alongside the drive, they were brought out only to hunt cougar in winter. They looked half-starved, though in fact they were half-poisoned from bi-weekly wormings. By the time Perry hunted his dogs, they inevitably ran off, and he would spend frenzied days tracking them through fresh snow in the mountains. When he found them, exhausted and nearly dead, dragging themselves toward home, he would worm them on the spot, pushing glue-filled gelatin pills against the backs of their tongues, then squeezing their muzzles until they swallowed.

And so, sad as it was, Perry's suicide in the dwindling light at the end of the year seemed anything but a surprise. He drove to his parents' ranch in his roadster, drove along the backside of the old homestead buildings to a pond circled by thick willows. He parked at the far end of the pond dam, backing his roadster into the thicket, where its orange flared like a hunter's fire on a distant ridge. He clamped a length of flexible tubing to the tailpipe, ran the tube into a garbage bag inside a burlap sack, which he tied tightly over his head. He was last seen alive filling up his roadster at a gas station in the valley. It was snowing lightly that afternoon. Perry had spent weeks collecting all the photographs of himself he could find, "For my life story," he told his wife. When they found the car, its engine stalled, its tank empty, Perry lay slumped over in the passenger's seat, his body dusted with snow, a pile of ashes at his feet.

❧❧

A week after Perry's funeral, Darwin and I decided to take Perry's daughters and my sons to cut Christmas trees. We planned, too, later that night, to drive them down to the general store to meet Santa Claus. So all six of us piled into Darwin's pickup and rattled over icy back roads to the tree farm.

The girls and my two boys, squished in between Darwin and me, focused anxiously on each approaching mailbox, "Is that it there? What's it say? Is that it ahead?" Round, freckled, loud, the younger of Perry's daughters, Twyla, still seemed unaffected by her father's death. But the older girl, Patty, her long hair far redder than her sister's, thin, freckled, quiet and withdrawn like her father, sat stoically beside her grandfather and watched the road wind ahead of her. That past week, the weight of what had happened to her had begun to sink deep as a dollop of lead dropped in a still, black pond. Already, a part of her beauty was becoming her reserve, the edge she was beginning to draw between herself and a world she would keep at a distance, even there in that cramped cab.

The tree farm covered a cleared slope at the base of Sunflower Mountain. What was pasture had been converted to rows of unpruned scotch pine and spruce. A lane led down from the road, along a corridor of dry knapweed, then under aspens that formed an arch over the ruts. An old woman came out of her trailer that was parked contingently on a flat space of frozen yellow clay bulldozed out of the steep slope above. She was the image, not of rural poverty, but of Presbyterian respectability, dressed in a wool skirt and knit blouse, her long grey braid tied in a knot at her nape. She told us to cut on the side of the hill directly above her trailer where the gangly pines grew in symmetrical rows. "When you find what you want, drag it down here and I'll measure." Without any more ceremony, she stepped back inside the trailer. Darwin limped beside me, and the children scattered like swallows down the weedy rows of trees.

We let them decide which trees to cut. And of course that took a long time. They debated over dozens. We crisscrossed the hillside, poised to cut one tree then another and another, but cut none. Impatient and tired after an hour, Darwin complained that his legs were "getting puny." So I insisted that each of the children choose one of the four trees we would cut, no further debate necessary or allowed. I dragged the trees down the lane to the trailer and the old woman reappeared, buttoning a neatly patched chore jacket. The afternoon sun had tilted to a flat angle out of the southwest, and the whole valley filled with a rich golden light. The pasture grass glistened green and silver, the frozen cess below the barn exploding with glare.

The old woman held her "measure stick" up beside our trees. Until Darwin winked at me and nodded the brim of his railroad cap at the stick, I had not noticed that the gradations were somewhat less than accurate. The first mark at waist height read "3 ft," and that seemed reasonable enough. But twelve inches above that the broad pencil mark read "5 ft 6 in." And six inches above that, "7 ft." All our trees were, guessing from her stick, taller than sixteen feet.

"Them trees are a little taller than average," she estimated. Darwin grinned and dickered a minute. That I could see over the top of each tree did little to discourage the old woman as she tallied the cost.

"Well, then," she concluded, generously, "I'll let you have that top two foot free. It being Christmas and all." Given the sizeable discount she was offering us for buying in bulk, her tally made the trees roughly equal to the price charged by her competitors, just a far better deal, when you thought about it. Then as a kind of afterthought to seal the deal, smiling with good big teeth, she asked, "Would you all like a cup of coffee?"

Darwin and I filed in behind her and the children disappeared into the barn. She poured yellow cream and sugared our cups without asking. Her husband and son had died two years earlier, while trimming the trees we just cut. They had taken their tractor straight up the steep slope in spring, and rolled it off the hillside onto themselves, breaking their necks. She told us this without prompting nor asking for pity. Hers was a world in which men killed themselves working. Darwin said he cut hay over there one year before her boy was old enough to drive a tractor. "Yes," she said, squinting one eye shut and looking Darwin over more closely, "I believe I do recall you now. You're Darwin's boy."

"We lived down along the highway then, across from the saw mill."

She nodded. In the warmth of her narrow kitchen, her cheeks reddened. The palms of her hands, turned up on the table, were deep with thick lines like the patterns on turtle shells that tell fortunes.

When we stood up to leave, dusk was well advanced. We pushed open the aluminum door and stepped out onto the landing above the frozen clay. "You boys know where to buy a tree next year. I need the business, so tell somebody. And I'll be seeing you." With that, she shoved the plywood door shut and a light flicked on in another room of her trailer. We called the children, who were in the barn, and a moment later pulled out of her lane onto the county road and followed the tunnel of our headlights over the ridge into the trees. It was darker in the canyon along Ashby Creek, an ice fog drifting among bare trees.

❧❧

That night we drove ten miles east from our road, toward the middle of the valley, where the village's main road winds past shabby farm houses and overgrown fields. We made a tight turn out of the scrub, and on our right a gas pump stood at the center of a clearing, lit by a single incandescent bulb that burned over the porch steps to the general store. The parking lot was full of battered automobiles and trucks. We bounced through frozen puddles and parked alongside a relic Econoline pickup.

My sons and Darwin's granddaughters suddenly began hanging back shyly. We nearly had to drag them through the door and down the aisles to the middle of the store, where, under one lit fluorescent tube, Santa Claus sat on an overturned crate. And it really was Santa Claus. This was no pillow-wearing, red felt-smocked, cottonball-bearded Santa. The man sitting there was the real deal: genuinely stout, his costume tailored from heavy flannel chamois cloth, with snowshoe rabbit fur trim. He wore black equestrian boots. His pipe filled the room with the sweet aroma of vanilla-flavored tobacco. But it was his shoulder-length and curly greying blonde hair, and long curly white beard that were most convincing. He was so convincing, in fact, that even the skeptical seven-year-olds who had seen the frauds across the river at the mall in Missoula, gaped at him, astonished and unwilling to step any closer, much less tell him their wish.

He sat there in the grey light, his back against the counter, the video poker machine, lottery tickets, and cigarette and beef jerky displays framing his rosy face. He gestured to the frightened children to gather around him and began speaking in a soft tenor, unlike any other voice I had ever heard in that valley. I was so taken with the man, I forgot about my own boys and Twyla and Patty. I wanted to laugh out loud and tell him I always knew he was for real, and that I knew the day would arrive when doubters and mockers would be revealed as the sad cases I had suspected they were all along.

"You children probably hope to get all the toys you've seen on the TV this year, and I hope you do, too," Old Man Claus began. "But I'm not sure I have some of those gifts with me in my sleigh this year. None of us should feel bitter about that, and your people can't help it if Santa can't keep up with the demand. Things just aren't like they used to be." Even then, among those children, there was a memory, a story that needed to be told, of a more prosperous past, call it a lie if you like, a lost but better world that defined their birthright as something more than what their lives would very likely allow. A remembered country of wealth and abundance: trees, water, minerals, grass, and game without end.

He stopped a moment to look at the owner of the store, who stepped out of the shadows. "Now you kids come on up here and tell Santa the one thing you want most this year." Of the dozen children in the store, only my boys and Darwin's granddaughters weren't from the village. Though they did not understand, this visit with Santa Claus did not really involve them—the poverty in that room was not ours to endure. There was a collection plate over by the door, and Darwin told me to leave whatever I could spare.

My boys clutched my legs and stared at Santa. I looked behind me, and Darwin's granddaughters stood together in the shadow at the far end of the aisle, surrounded by shining soup cans and bright foil bags of chips. Long red hair hung in their faces and they peered at me, afraid I would gesture to them, urging them forward into the light.

❧❧

Driving home over the dark hills, I remembered Halley's Comet was in the sky that night in the southeast above Jupiter. We were back in the National Forest above Ashby Creek. Darwin said he knew a good spot to stop and see the sky. We bounced down washboard roads under the bare aspens and larches. Darwin pulled off onto a side road, parked and set the hand brake. Then we walked along a wide two-track into a potato field.

I found Jupiter without any trouble and held my fist in the air above the planet, trying to sight the comet. Those past weeks I had wished for some sign, an image of hope to redeem those children, their families, the plundered mountains. Every morning, when I looked out at Nye Escue's wheat field, it was clear how a man keeps his faith alive, and I wanted the girls to see themselves as green and thriving as those fields, even at that darkest time of year, the darkest moment of their young lives. Given the wealth that was raped from those mountains, what more hope could we offer them than the inheritance implied by the image of recurrence in a wheat field, a healing world? But I could not find anything to call a comet, or tell them anything more convincing than the miracle of renewal we were searching for in the sky that night was a pale sphere of blue light—there!—barely visible, returning as if from some near extinction.

The Fidelity of Thieves

forgiveness, if it comes, comes from a honeycomb of tenderness

—John Berger

S ince the August morning we left Montana, I have heard nothing about the bees we kept there. Then yesterday a package arrived in the mail that started me thinking again about my brief history as a beekeeper and thief. As soon as I read the return address, I knew what Bill had sent at last. I called my sons to come quick, try a taste of our bees' honey. They have no recollection of what I could possibly be talking about. Bees? I lifted the plastic pop bottles full of amber honey from the popped corn that Bill used as packing material. And then they were laughing with me, each dipping his right index finger and having a lick. The honey tasted of the brief, intense Montana bloom: balsamroot, daisy, wild iris, wild rose, chokecherry, plum, huckleberry, mint— the infinity of wildflowers that blossom in the foothills that surround Bill's ranch. When Josefa appeared later in the day at the far end of the street, walking home, we rushed out to greet her, bearing one of the bottles aloft like nectar offered to the gods. And met her in the middle of the intersection. We stood in the street, a confabulation of enthusiasts, confirming our neighbors' doubts about our dignity and sanity, loudly celebrating that sweet, crushingly lovely, and perishing Montana summer.

༄༄

I started keeping bees unintentionally. All I said to my neighbor one spring afternoon as we sat sharing a smoke was that the orchard was full of bees working the bloom: "I think that would make good honey."

In a downpour two nights later, Darwin rattled up the lane in his pickup. "I brought you some bees, Dave. If you want them."

I knew already from experience that Darwin had probably stolen the bees. I could guess how and from where he had stolen them. There were hobby ranches along the side roads in the valley. Their owners lived in Spokane, Portland, and Seattle. They had purchased the dilapidated homesteads when the agricultural economy was worse than usual. These absentee owners practiced their own forms of nostalgia: many of them had lived in Montana when they were children, when it was still a union state, before the economy collapsed and its politicians and citizens began further debasing themselves to satisfy the will of corporate interests. So their second homes were an effort to reclaim a heritage that had long ago vanished from the earth, leaving behind it only the poisoned industrial wounds of better times than the present. They remodeled pioneer-era cabins, re-chinked the exterior walls, rebuilt fences, and then bought a few head of cattle (usually of an exotic variety), sold a few tons of hay—just enough to generate a "farm income" and therefore losses sufficient to earn a tax break. The hobby ranchers seldom visited their bad investments—usually just for a few weeks in late summer, accompanied by their bored or over-eager families, whose clean, pressed farm clothes were newly purchased from mail-order catalogs. Those few weeks aside, their property was prey to local foragers who, like Darwin, had been hired to oversee the ranches in their owners' extended absence.

Darwin's fishing pond, for example. One spring morning he asked if I would be interested in some good fishing. We drove over a low ridge and down along a fork of the stream that feeds his own pond. He had four fifty-five-gallon drums we took a long time to fill with water from the creek and that sloshed around in the bed of his truck. Then we headed toward the ranch of an absentee owner. The fencerows, ditches, and pastures were clear of weeds, the fences tight, the woodlots "scientifically thinned and managed," but not a human soul was anywhere in sight. We pulled up below the pond dam, Darwin gunned the engine of his truck and raced up the slick grass to the shore. I looked back at the steaming tire tracks that scarred the deep orchard grass. "You know the guy that owns this place?"

"Oh sure," Darwin said.

We crimped the barbs on our hooks and cast our lines, but Darwin also had brought along trot-lines, and four additional poles, as well as his spinning rod. In no time the brook trout started to hit. Every fish he landed, Darwin reeled in, gently unhooked, and tossed over his shoulder into one of the fifty-five-gallon barrels. After a couple of hours, during which we must have emptied the pond of brook trout, including several bloody-bellied behemoths, I asked Darwin if he thought we had reached our limit. "Well, I tell you what, Dave: there's still a mess of fish to be caught yet." Soon we were at another pond, employing the same democratic methods. By noon, when I crawled up into the bed of the truck and had a look in the barrels, I was flabbergasted. There were so many trout, the surface literally boiled with their fins and curving iridescent sides.

So the evening of the downpour, when I heard Darwin offer me hives of bees, I knew exactly what I was getting into. What do you say to a man with a truck full of hives, pilfered or not? I stood on the porch, rain beating the metal roof, and shouted, "What the hell do you want me to do with them?"

He backed his pickup around to my garage under the house and shouted up through the porch floor, "Come on down, Dave. I'll show you what we got here." In addition to the stolen hives, Darwin brought along his father's old rotten bee boxes. He pulled these out of the corner of the truck bed and began explaining about frames, wax foundations, smokers, veils, brood boxes, excluders, and supers. I had no idea what any of this meant but knew that, like most of Darwin's schemes that included me, this was going to cost me something. Soon, he exhausted his knowledge and we stood side by side, mutely staring at the pile of rotting hives, the bees sealed inside the boxes filling the basement with a soft, but nervous hum.

ᘒᘒ

The morning after the arrival of my bees, I went to the cellar to scrub the walls of the empty hives with cottonwood leaves so that they would not become "foul brooded," as Darwin said. Although I did not know what "foul brooded" meant, I knew I did not want it. I then cleaned, repaired, and painted the boxes. Using scrap lumber, I built and painted new bottom boards and bee entrances. Then went to the feed store for wax foundations and pins to fit into the frames. Finally I smoked the bees out of their old hives, moved the old frames and brood cells to the repaired hives, and watched astounded as the bees poured into the new boxes. On top of these, between the deep supers and the shallow honey supers with "pound sections" (my future take of honey), I slipped in excluders—really just a barbecue grill with cross-wires close enough together that only the workers could squeeze through, but not the egg-laying queen. Within an hour, workers began launching from the bottom boards of the hives to work the last of the honey flow in our orchard. Darwin, who had come by to see how I was getting on, sat with me on the bank above what he kept calling "our" beeyard, sharing a smoke. "I tell you what, Dave, that's going to make us some real mellow honey."

Within weeks, Darwin had another scheme. His son had been out poaching in the forest along Ashby Creek and said there was a wild swarm at the head of the draw, just above the lower pasture. "You find the queen," Darwin said with the confidence of a used-car salesman, "you'd have yourself another good hive of bees." All we had to do was take the smoker and veil, a chainsaw, an adze, and another box of frames and foundations out to the woods in the morning when it would still be cool, cut down the snag, split it open, find the queen (he assured me again that this would be easy), then put her in the box. The rest of the colony would follow.

"Have you ever done this before?" I asked. No, he had never captured a wild hive, but had heard his father describe it when he was a boy.

I did not offer to help.

The next morning though, he showed up at dawn with his chainsaw. "You got the box ready, Dave?"

No, I didn't, and he drove away.

The following morning, however, I did, and off we went in his pickup down the Forest Service road a short distance, and into the forest. We parked and hauled our gear no more than fifty yards down through second-growth pines near the creek. There stood a fifteen-foot-tall snag full of woodpecker holes. Only a few bees swarmed around a small opening about halfway up; and a few workers returned with full pollen baskets hanging from their hind legs despite the cool air. These, it turned out, were wild bees, or Italian bees gone wild, and far less docile than my Caucasian bees, around whom already I could stand unveiled when I opened their hives to inspect their work. As we approached, defender bees buzzed by, warning us off. But Darwin, limping determinedly toward the tree on his bad leg, choked the chainsaw, pulled the cord, and waded up to the base of the snag, a blue cloud of burnt oil filling the air, while I veiled myself and lit the smoker.

No sooner had the snag cracked and fallen when Darwin limped off to a safe distance, saying, "She's all yours, Dave!" The snag thumped into the deep forest duff and bees spilled out. They were on me in an instant. I stood there, sweat flooding every pore of my body under two layers of clothes and winter parka, a cloud of bees striking wherever they thought they had a chance to reach flesh.

The idea was to split the snag in two with my adze, open the hive, pick out the queen and drop her in the deep super I had hauled down the hill. We'd leave the honeycomb for the bears.

With a cloud of angry defenders sacrificing themselves trying to drill me, I began at the base of the fallen snag and split it length-wise along the grain. I had never before split an entire tree down the middle, but the trunk was dry and punky, and the process proved easy enough. Straddling the long trunk, I raised the heavy blade and—thwak, thwak—a crack began to open in the tree between my legs. I passed the hive entrance, inciting the bees again, and worked my way up toward the end of the snag. I said to Darwin, "You don't suppose that this snag is going to fall apart into two even halves, do you?"

"Sure, Dave," he said. "Happens every time." He was hiding behind a big ponderosa pine sixty feet up the slope, smoking a generic menthol, and casting a wary eye at the air all around him. I reached the end of the snag, raised my adze one last time and—pthunk!—the snag fell open like a book. And there, curled between my legs, just wakened in its nest of soft dry needles, witches beard, and leaves was a fat, bedazzled rattlesnake.

I screamed, stunned, staring down between my legs.

"Y'ought not to let it bite off your tallywhacker, Dave!" Apparently this was great fun for Darwin. I pivoted away on one leg and stepped up the slope, breathless, and crumpled, my legs firm as rubber bands.

Darwin crushed out his cigarette on the trunk of the ponderosa pine. I said, "What do you think I ought to do now?"

"Kill it, Dave." He said this so matter-of-factly that I actually stood and took one determined step down the slope toward the snake. Still too stiff itself from the morning cold to flee, it lay there watching, and waiting for my decision. But then I looked at the absurdly short handle of the adze in my hand and it occurred to me that I would have to step well within the snake's own striking range if I hoped to kill it.

Also, I recently had had a bad experience with a snake. It had startled me one day as I was walking down the basement stairs and came eyeball to eyeball with it on the sill of the sunroom. I tried to pick it up with a stick but the slender tip bowed and the snake slipped off, dropping with a small thud under the stairs and into the cellar. I might have left well enough alone then: there were rats in our cellar anyway, so my snake had come, old god of the pantry, to assist a gruesome task in the potato bins. For its part, that snake wished only to warm itself on the bright glassed-in porch, then return to making its useful living, quietly, in the cellar. But I hurried to the barn, fetched a hoe, which the snake understood, coiling itself tighter under the stairs, wishing I would give up my pitiful fear. But I goaded the snake, tried to drag it from its lair, took an awkward chop and missed. The snake reared in the air, hissing, mouth gaping, it lunged in one fatal convulsion, closing the distance between knowledge and its death. I brought the hoe down fast, precisely at the point where the spine attaches to the skull, watched the body go limp as a rope, then kicked the head aside, rats squeaking nervously in the gloom.

Still ashamed of myself for my action that day, I had no intention whatsoever of killing that rattlesnake in the forest. I picked up a long, stout limb, pushed it under the body of the rattler, then tossed him like an old inner-tube down the hillside into the duff, where he landed like a grunting weight, then suddenly was gone.

Now there were only the angry bees to tend. The wild hive spread along half the length of the snag. Brood cells and honey cells, too, were dispersed haphazardly throughout those seven and a half feet of the trunk. The hive followed exactly the erratic, rotted contours of the hollow tree. It was not as simple as finding the cluster of workers who comprised the royal court and then snatching away their queen, the entire colony in pursuit. I had to excavate the hive as clumsily as a bear, splitting away pieces of wood with the adze, scooping out brood cells, covering my hands and arms with wax and honey. It was a gross violation, and so infuriating to the bees that as many bees as I killed, searching for their queen, died imbedding their stingers in the fabric of my clothes, the outside layer of which was dotted with uprooted stingers and tiny dewdrops of venom.

At last, I found the queen deep inside the hive, surrounded by a fist of attendants. Now, how exactly did I expect to pick her up? With thick, sticky gloves I could not so much as zip the fly of my overalls (which I had forgotten to do), much less pick up that delicate queen. As in all actions worthy of our humanity, I had to take off my gloves and use my naked hands.

When I picked her up, expecting to be attacked, nothing at all happened. There she was between my right thumb and forefinger—small, soft, and warm. It was a vast moment of tenderness, in spite of what preceded it.

"By God, I got her, Darwin!" I whispered and placed her in the middle frame in the white box beside me. A moment later, as though all had been forgiven, the remaining bees flowed after her into the hive.

❧❧

The bees were productive despite my incompetence, and they were tolerant of my presence once I acquired the common wisdom of not approaching or passing in the front of the hive. Since my violent raid on the wild hive, I had not been stung again. My bees and I were at peace with one another, and they permitted me to "work" the hive, checking brood for disease and storage cells for uniformity, without making it necessary for me to wear either gloves or veil. This seemed like a privilege they had granted. Having forgiven my ignorance, they allowed me a probationary period during which they would regard my work as an older man might patiently watch the work of his apprentice.

Nevertheless, my bees were costing more than I could afford. The expense of foundation frames, wax foundations, and foundation pins, not to mention the repair of Darwin Sr.'s old hives and the cost of new hive kits, busted my bee account long before I ever considered buying a honey extractor, which is what I needed more than ever in order to taste the blossom of the preceding year. It was time to harvest the strong, dark honey. And perhaps, I argued to Josefa, the excess honey could be sold to cover some of my costs. A ploy, by the way, that she didn't for a moment believe, and nixed my scheme.

Reluctant to bother my bees in the fall, when they worked feverishly to gather the last honey flow from the asters, I put off harvesting my honey too long. It was almost Christmas. Of course, this should have been done much earlier, whenever the bees completed filling a super of chunk honey or pound sections. I knew the shallow supers had been full for months. But chastened by the violence of getting the bees in the first place, I was reluctant to take anything away from them, and considered my reticence the basis of our mutual accommodation. I waited a long time and reasoned that, given the cooler weather, the bees would be clustered in the deep super and therefore leave me alone when I jerked the honey supers away.

But how was I going to get the honey out of the hive and into jars? I did not dare ask Darwin. Obviously, he was as ignorant of methods as I, but his ignorance would seek a solution in my gullible wallet. I couldn't afford the expense of the fancy stainless-steel honey extractor.

One evening near the solstice when the beeyard was full of moonlight, I went out to the hives and began taking off the honey. In spite of all the mistakes I had already made, and was making at that moment, the sheer weight of those honey supers delighted me. Each weighed at least twenty-five pounds. I carried them one at a time across the frozen meadow to the house and piled them up on the kitchen counter.

At first we tried to split the combs lengthwise with a hot knife slipped along the foundation, then drain them upside down on bread racks near the woodstove. But at the end of an hour, precious little honey had drained into pans. We then filled a big stock pot with combs, turned up the heat, melted the wax, and hoped that it would separate from the honey. Then we could skim off the wax and pour the clear honey into jars. It was a fabulous idea, but by the time the second hive was melted and skimmed, Josefa had gone to bed and I was left with one hundred and fifty pounds of deep red honey poured into every bowl, pan, and pot we possessed. Standing over the big canner, I stared down into the warm honey.

I could not resist. I plunged my hands up past the wrists into that warm, sticky abundance of honey. Having done virtually everything wrong up to that point, so why not this, too? One of the oddest pleasures was pulling my hands out, making fists, and squeezing the honey between my fingers and against my palms. Then I washed my hands in the honey, rubadubdub, until my skin glistened golden-red. With a spatula, I finally scraped most of the honey from my hands, licked them, then washed them in cold water to allow the still unseparated wax to congeal and stiffen around my fingers. I washed out dozens of half-gallon mason jars and gallon milk jugs, skimmed the wax as best I could, poured the honey, and finally went to bed to dream of flecks of wax like embryos floating as in the thick amber light of the womb.

In spite of all the errors I made, in spite of it all, the bees flourished. By May of the following year I confronted a new problem: the bees were doing far too well. I couldn't keep up with their rate of reproduction. I bought all the hive kits I could afford, but my hives continued to grow too crowded. And because I never looked for or thought to destroy new queen cells, every few weeks, bees would begin swarming around the entrance of a hive and covering the sides and lid. Then, as soon as a new queen emerged from the hive, off they went in search of a snag in the forest, or—because the outside walls of our house were riddled with missing insulation plugs from the time the insulation crew winterized it—they built their hives in any open space they could find between studs in the walls of our old farmhouse. We walked from room to room, our ears pressed to plaster, listening to the soft hum of bees dancing in the darkness between the walls.

Hive after hive put off a swarm, but I was never able to find a single one of these swarms before it set up its household elsewhere. It was just as well, since I had only one more empty box of frames and foundations anyway. Ashamed by my lack of preparation, and given the dubious circumstances under which I had come by all these bees, I felt criminally negligent, wasteful, and stupid.

As I returned one afternoon from a hike on Diamond Mountain, I heard Josefa calling from the porch, "Look in the honey locusts in back of the barn!"

There, hanging from a bowed limb was what looked like a six-foot-long sturgeon. The most recent swarm had not fled far from its hive. It was almost within reach; if I stood on a chair I could easily cut the limb with pruning shears, and then shake the swarm from the limb into my last box. This was an opportunity (perhaps) to redeem myself. I hustled into action. Despite the heat and the docile nature of swarming bees, I decided to put on my veil, overalls, and heavy gloves. I carried the empty box from the barn over to the beeyard, and placed a chair under the swarm. The limb they clung to was not so much as a twig, but the swarm itself was perhaps ten inches wide. The bees were clinging to each other!

As I reached above my head with the pruning shears, it never occurred to me that the swarm might actually be heavy. I dropped the bees. I didn't just drop them, either; I dropped them on my head.

It was an eerie sensation with all those bees covering my face and shoulders. They were not angry, not in the least. They just clustered up again, calmly gathering into a globe of gently vibrating wings around my head. Josefa gasped.

"Oh my god!" I said from inside the swarm. Though I couldn't see, I assumed from my family's muffled laughter that I must have appeared somewhat ridiculous. Josefa offered to fetch the bee book and read to me what I should do next. I agreed, that was a very good idea.

"It says here the bees likely won't sting while they're swarming." I heard her flipping madly through the pages of the Extension Service pamphlet. " 'Shake the bees off on the alighting board,' " she read, and paused. "Now that's a problem," she said, stopping to consider how, given my covered face and eyes, I would find the hive, much less shake the bees off my head before its entrance. "I think I'm going to have to lead you to the hive, dear." I heard her step over into the locust grove and pick up the limb on which the swarm had initially alighted. "It says that 'once shaken before the hive entrance, the swarm will enter in the most enthusiastic way.' Here," she poked me with the locust limb. "Be careful not to grab hold of a thorn."

So in this way, each of us grasping one end of the limb, Josefa led me slowly across the lawn to the beeyard. Once in front of the empty hive, I knelt before the bottom board and groped to locate the entrance to the hive, then gave my head a stiff jerk. The bees slipped off me like mud from a shovel blade. They hit the grass in front of the hive entrance and, following their queen, they poured inside. Three minutes later, not a single bee remained outside the hive. Several more minutes passed and field bees began launching from the alighting board, heading off in search of pollen, beginning to build their new hive.

We sat together on the lawn, all four of us—Josefa and I and our sons—and laughed until we laughed ourselves into silence. The bees darted to and from the hives like sparks of gold light. They were working the locust blossoms in the grove behind us, where Ezra pointed our attention: four saw-whet owls, standing side-by-side deep in the mottled shadows, watched our curious goings on from a limb of a honey locust tree.

❧❧

We knew all along that we would leave Montana. The summer that followed the capture of the swarm would be our last there. Now I had another problem. Because of the ongoing marijuana wars being waged by many of the unemployed young men in the valley that summer, I kept my distance from Darwin, knowing there was always a danger of being stopped somewhere by one of his paranoid rivals. Gunfire sounded in the foothills day and night. Darwin was so busy guarding his marijuana patches and those of his allies, he never thought to ask what I would do with "our" bees when we moved to Oregon in August. Leaving them with Darwin was the worst option. The hives his father had left after he died fell quickly into disrepair and finally vanished into weeds and scrub. I thought maybe I would haul the bees across the mountains to Oregon, but that was ridiculous. The summer had been one of the hottest in memory. Then the state announced a quarantine on all bee hives because of the widespread presence of a mite that destroyed brood cells. My hives appeared healthy in that regard, but I knew I must leave them behind.

I met another beekeeper at the feed store when we both were there to buy foundations. "So you're the one," an older man said, and left me wondering precisely what that might mean. The one other beekeeper in the valley? The one who had stolen bees? The one associated with the scurrilous Darwin? Whatever the meaning, he accepted me into the fraternity of beekeepers at the moment I would be leaving it.

Bill had kept a small beeyard for years. He had an actual job (in the P.O.), which meant that he could better afford the cost of maintaining the hives. We became friends, stopping whenever we saw each other driving along the dirt roads in the valley to compare what we'd recently observed in our beeyards. We agreed that I would prepare the hives for him, close them off, move them down to the lane, where he could load them into his truck. This I would do the night before we moved. I had not anticipated any problems, really, though of course a familiar pattern quickly established itself. The hives were too crowded. Again. The bees could not be coaxed into their hives because there was no more room for them inside. What was I going to do? I stuffed the entrances to the hives with straw, leaving only a small opening, no wider than two bees could pass—one entering, one exiting simultaneously. The improbable idea was that the bees, seeing this gesture of imminent transport, would understand the consequences of being left behind, and would, thus, jam themselves all into the hive.

Before dawn, I went out to look at the hives, and only one was not covered with bees, longing to get inside. I left a note stuck to the waxy tin of one of the hive lids: "Sorry, Bill, they don't seem to appreciate my good intentions." We climbed up into our rented moving truck, emblazoned with the cursive slogan, "Move it yourself," and pulled down the long lane to the county road. That was the last I ever saw of my bees.

ℒℒ

A week after the honey arrived in Oregon, a letter came from Bill, beginning, "I assume by now you've received the honey." When he had come to pick up the hives, he had fussed with the bees, too, trying to coax them inside, but without any luck. "The great congregation on the hives would not return to the hive," he wrote, "so I lifted the whole thing into the bed of the truck and drove off. Not much else to do. Kept watching them and the little critters stayed with the flow." That stream of bees followed behind him for ten miles to his ranch. "I worried only that I'd drive past someone whose car window was open. But no problem."

When he arrived at his beeyard, Bill unloaded, removed the shallow supers—which were loaded with honey—and put on new brood boxes. "In a few days all the bees were working inside the hives. They survived the heat and the parasites of that summer, and even after a minus twenty-six degree morning in December, they didn't croak either."

I took a quart of the honey that Bill sent from Montana to a friend here in Oregon who had kept bees at one time, too—a family tradition going back two generations, a skill he had learned from his grandfather, who kept "migratory hives" that they moved, a couple hundred hives at a time, on the back of a flatbed truck, following the first bloom east of the Washington Cascades into the apple country along the Wenatchee and Okanogan rivers. He has shared the last of his own harvest with me for the past two years—big crystallized gallon jars of honey. He now shared my own much stronger and darker harvest. I had pretended to him I was a beekeeper once, lying about my own skill, all my stories revised to reflect what I have read about in the beekeeping books I never bothered to read while I still kept bees. We have talked about working bees together. But I think not. There is no point in another such partnership, especially one that is a response to our mutual nostalgia for a practice that we never mastered so much as we were mastered by it. The only virtue in our proposed scheme: it would not be predicated on the theft of anyone's "abandoned" hives.

And besides, there is another beekeeper in town whose beeyards are scattered about the valley and who sells honey from a stand in front of his house. Each beeyard produces its own distinct honey— from dark red and richly flavored to a more subtly flavored and wheat-colored honey. He is a calm and quiet man who chooses his words with tremendous care, and is comfortable with long silences in conversation. If he, too, is a thief, then only in the most highly refined sense of that word. His fidelity to bees is of an entirely greater magnitude than my own.

Last year the spring bloom was so brief and summer so dry his bees could barely provide enough honey to sustain themselves. When I knocked at his door in the fall his son explained that he and his father had not taken any honey, but instead had fed their bees all summer and would have to continue nursing the hives all winter just to save them from starvation, if disease didn't kill off the weakened colonies first. And so if all went well there would be no honey until next year.

The beekeeper's son, a grown man, has Down's Syndrome and despite this has learned to work at father's side among the bees. I have watched them together as they move in their veils slowly among the hives with what seems, from a distance, a tremendous tenderness that has more to do with the sweetness of their love and fidelity toward their bees and each other than for the honey the bees may provide in more abundant years. Honey, I have learned, is not the point of beekeeping any more than the sweetness of nostalgia is the point of storytelling, a narrative that somehow makes our lives more orderly or meaningful than they might otherwise have been. Honey, like a story, is all that remains, that portion of our lives for which we have been granted yet another reprieve, forgiven for our poverty, our frailty, our heedlessness and error.

April Fools

the truths of outrage,
the truths of possibility

—Muriel Rukeyser

A glorious morning. Two below zero in Bear Creek Canyon at dawn. The spring storm that dragged cold air out of Canada in its wake left three inches of snow on top of the remaining two feet of hardpack that had repeatedly melted and re-frozen into alternating layers of corn snow and ice. The fitful end of a Montana winter. After the light's long absence, the sun having wandered away on its low curve south of the Sapphire Mountains, we now celebrate its return, its familiar clarity and warmth, knowing such light after long darkness is elixir. We feel as wild and easily led astray as Nebuchadnezzar. If there were grass instead of snow, we would roll in it like dogs, luxuriate in its lushness, push our shoulder blades like plows into its thick exuberances, sloughing the dry itch of winter from our skin. But it is, after all, two below zero, and sun or no sun, we restrain ourselves, bundled up as warmly as if it were still December. Tomorrow is the first of April, the Feast of Fools.

Below us, Bear Creek overruns its banks and floods the pasture. But because of the cold, it forms a sheet of ice in the creek bottom, cut here and there by rivulets that pour across the surface accumulating thin, brittle layers of ice. Under our feet, water hisses, too, finding its way down the canyon toward the Big Blackfoot. Crossing a fence at the far end of the pasture, the ranch boundary, we head uphill, through a mixed forest of Douglas fir, a few ponderosa, cottonwood, alder, and mountain ash. The forest we walk in, though owned by a timber conglomerate, has always seemed an intimate part of the Bear Creek Ranch. The forest just south of our friends' house is land—but for the surveyor's geometry—indistinguishable from the ranch, the canyon, and the ridge that rises above. When the snow is gone in late April, the trail that follows the stream above Bear Creek Ranch is deep in russet needles and bright green moss. By May, there are Calypso orchid, pipsissewa, wintergreen, and kinnickinnick, each thriving in the soft slough of the forest floor. It is a place that is quick to suggest its potential for pleasure. Josefa and I made love here one brief summer long ago, as I suppose our friends have. To acknowledge legal boundaries here would violate the expansiveness of our affections for each other and for the place itself.

Above the wide creek bottom, where the canyon narrows, the trail soon joins a logging road. Above that road, fifteen years ago, another timber conglomerate, who then owned the property on the other side of the fence line we just crossed, stripped the mountainside in two weeks in late July. We sat in the pasture and watched men fall trees and drag them straight down the mountain along dozens of skid trials that soon began to erode and silt in the creek below. Five years later, the creek would need "rehabilitation," like a young criminal, Fish and Game footing the bill to restore the spawning beds of brown trout and Dolly Varden that once grew here to the size of one's arm from elbow to wrist. But fifteen years ago, mistaking this bottomland of old trees as our own, we thought, there's no more timber here—that commodifying noun form for "forest." If we live long enough, we thought then, we'll see something at least like a forest again on this mountainside.

Such "forests," however, are more like retirement homes or grade levels at school, segregated by age, and unlike extended families, with their complicated mix of the young, the middle-aged, the elderly, and the dead who lay underground. The industrial forest is perhaps an unlikely but acute metaphor of personal and familial fragmentation—what we have done to the forest, we have done to ourselves, our families, and our communities.

From the porch, as I laced my boots and soaked in the warmth of the spring sun, I saw across the creek bottom that the crowns of the old fir trees were golden brown with a thick crop of cones. Perhaps such luxurious growth is merely random. Perhaps it is the potential of mature trees. Perhaps it results from the record wetness of the past year, the first in a predicted twenty-year trend toward wetter, cooler weather.

Or perhaps, as I suspected, the trees are as aware of their predicament as we are this morning, walking the day before the tree-fallers arrive.

ꙮꙮ

Josefa and I have not lived at Bear Creek for the past fifteen years, and in fact, only lived here very briefly, not two full years. Until he was four, our youngest child had never seen the broad hayfield full of daisies in June, tilting downward toward Bear Creek; and though its image faded from the color snapshots in the family album, it was nevertheless vivid in the stories he heard. Bear Creek Canyon remains the geographic center of our imagined lives. We became young adults here, made the transition from childhood to parenthood, and first encountered something of the grave awareness of grown men and women coming face to face for the first time with the limitations of their lives. There is a dangerously seductive moment in one's mid-twenties, not unlike certain moments in childhood, when it seems that anything can happen— death, disappointment, or grace—and this moment will shape years to come. Yet this fails to describe that brief time spent at Bear Creek because this description, too, seems grandiose, thick with a whiff of nostalgia. Even so, Bear Creek was the geography of that crucial moment, and became greater in imagination than it might otherwise have been in ordinary experience.

Once we moved away from Bear Creek, to a valley farther west, where virtually every inch of soil has been disturbed by human desires, this canyon, perceived in memory as inviolate as the morning of creation, became the main character in the stories we told, stories that attached themselves to us by virtue of the intensity of our feeling for what Robinson Jeffers called "this fate going on outside our fate." That is the one true thing to tell about our time at Bear Creek. Despite the inflation of memory and its nostalgic egotisms, humility became the basic assumption of our relations to any place, the seed bed from which our lives would continue to grow. Humility directed toward lives other than our own, respect for the intimacy of knowledge others possessed of a place. And that intensity of feeling for what is alive besides ourselves often alienated us from people we met elsewhere who had never experienced such an intensity, and were suspicious even of its possibility.

A pair of nesting herons; a herd of horses stampeding past a cabin on a moonlit January night; a solemn-faced bear turning from the aspen tree she is scratching with her claws to ponder us pondering her; the Northern Lights shooting from the horizon to the zenith in flares of magenta, emerald, and silver; ten elk running south across the pasture at dawn; a pair of golden eagles circling our garden on the day we wed; wolves straying across the border out of Canada, howling one night then vanishing, leaving only tracks in the snow. . . living at a great distance from Bear Creek, these remembered presences haunted us, though for others, they were little more than the fanciful, dull, untamed drone of a young couple whose words lacked the decorous, recognizable shapes of human design.

Which was exactly the incommunicable point.

Our silence and isolation through two winters in Bear Creek Canyon became the filter through which all other experiences would be judged, the essential knowledge we carried away from that place. Our lives were not the only lives. It seems ridiculously simple. And perhaps even this grander claim: human lives are not the sole lives on which consciousness is predicated. It seemed obvious enough to us, though everywhere we looked this was denied by the actions of others. And so it seemed, in the years immediately after we left Bear Creek, we inhabited a brutalized landscape that regarded us and our kind with nothing short of a malevolent glare.

Our fantasy of exile seemed absolute, and return impossible. The wheel, set in motion, would revolve so ponderously it would never complete a cycle in our allotted years. Soon, of course, we did return. Though at first only in these repugnant fantasies. Like starving ghosts, we went begging with empty rice bowls. Remaining stoned for four years, I spent entire weeks living elsewhere in my mind. Then, finally, we closed the circle many times, though visits were often colored by an imagined dimension of tragic irony, as though we could no longer see what we had witnessed here long before. That static place in memory had, in reality, changed, and not for the better. New roads cutting willy-nilly though the valley, the hillsides stripped of trees, monster houses in every clearing—Bear Creek had come to resemble the brutalized landscapes we wandered across during our exile. "Irony is," as Barbara Guest has said, "the coagulant of pain," and thus, it seems now, that initial irony, with which we regarded Bear Creek soon after our return, was necessary before we could actually return, healed.

Two years ago, I drove three hundred miles through just-plowed fields in the northeastern Oregon valley where I live now, patterns of frost swirling wherever the plow turned; then wound through the whitewater gorges of the Clearwater and Lochsa rivers, crossed the Bitterroots, and followed the Big Blackfoot River east until I reached Bear Creek, where I parked, and walked into the canyon on foot at midnight. My old neighbor's dogs greeted me at the cattle grate as the horned May moon set in clouds. Bear Creek was loud with run-off; Diamond Mountain a dark hump in silhouette against the lighter blue of the sky. I had floundered for years, found myself there by chance alone, a mile up the same narrow, familiar road to the interior of my life, accepted, if not recognized by those three dogs, who, like guardians, had fallen into formation around me, leading the way. The years were gone, and I felt strangely ashamed, recalling that prior time, still more vivid than any other I had known since, when each incident seemed a sign, the significance of which I hardly knew how to read, less how to be guided by or changed.

Tramping through the snow the last cold morning in March, I want to put the fate of the trees out of my mind. The forested bottomland has not fallen to the saw in longer than a human lifetime. But the blue slashes of the timber cruiser's spray paint on the trunks of the trees is unmistakably clear. So I keep my eyes low to the ground, and in doing so, understand the intentions of these trees. The fresh snow is covered by a layer of amber seeds that swirled down from the dense clusters of cones that had just opened in the sun. Seeds lie all around me, from one side of the trail to the other, below the snowberry shrubs and the alders, and lie thickest upon the snow in fifty-foot-wide circles around the bases of the firs at the edge of the meadow. An incipient forest, albeit a forest of a single generation, a forest of uniform trees. Hardly a forest at all if one believes that a forest is more than a crop of uniformly marketable trees and a few invasive, opportunistic weeds. A forest I will never see as I have seen this one. The trees, determined to going on living the only way possible, have accepted the tree fallers' conditions.

And now I hear the birds. Hundreds. They are so loud in that cold air, I feel a moment of embarrassment that I had not been aware of them sooner, so much louder was the outrage in me that I would never walk in this place again. The tree tops swarm with flocks of pine siskins, feasting on the seeds. What they miss they shake down onto the forest floor. An amber rain of seeds, enough for everyone that last day before another part of the life we share scatters.

What is the alternative?

Sane as the Mind
that Makes a Nest

Crossing a fence, I straightened and came eye to eye with a female robin, who sat on her nest in the crook of a limb. The nest and the feathers of her back were the precise color of the bark of the fir tree where she had woven her refuge: slate-blue. She seemed so intently present in this place or confident of my human hurried-ness, she was not tempted to budge. In the split-second our gazes met, she must have been wondering what it was I saw, if in fact I saw at all. Was she invisible as she intended? But no sooner than our eyes made contact, she spilled from the nest and vanished. She was right—I saw her, but had I actually seen her the moment before she startled up with a flicker of her wing and rowed the air into the forest?

Days later, after a windstorm, I had forgotten about her nest; passing along the same trail and stepping across the barbed-wire fence once again, I found the nest on the forest floor and picked it up. Three broken blue eggs lay inside, the once-warm yellow jelly of the yolks cold and almost dry. This disaster aside, the nest was an ingeniously made thing. It consisted of three nests! The outer was woven of the roughest slough she and her mate had gleaned from the forest, but the nest within this outer nest was woven of soft, dry flowers of arrowood, whose blossoms had hung in white clusters almost a year earlier, in July. And this second nest was lined with yet another nest of reddish down she and her mate must have removed from their own breasts.

This past winter, whenever I happened upon them, I photographed bird nests in the trees and shrubs where they had been built and then abandoned. There was very little aesthetic intention in the photos, no attempt at composing images: the nest is right there at the center of each frame. A snapshot: a record, but not art. And that is all the photographer wished for: a picture demonstrating little more skill of seeing than what a passing glance reveals. Impatient, how else do we know the world? We use the photograph in a conventional manner, require memory to reconstruct from the object its context, and the narrative in which it is embedded. This is perhaps the best most of us can hope for. Just as, seeing the robin at the moment she fled her nest, hadn't I invented her camouflaged presence there in the nest in the crook of the fir tree that moment just prior to actually seeing?

In my pictures, at the center of the frame, there are large nests woven of coarse grass and sedge, dry stems of wildflowers, russet pine needles, and various shades of mud, constructed just out of reach in alders and young firs. The smaller nests are unobtrusively placed deep in hawthorn and floribunda thickets, and woven of modest, ingenious stuff: strands of moss, fine grass, witches beard, wolfbait; and are so vulnerable, after winter storms, they are sometimes blown far from their sanctuaries of thorns, and lie in an up-ended heap along a trail or in meadowgrass. These I carry home and place on a shelf, at either end of which are baskets. Between the baskets on the shelf, and to which I add the nests, is a collection of turtle shells, wasp nests, earthstars, a red-tailed hawk's claw, a mouse's skull, the curved beak of a curlew, a red clay pot packed full of feathers—all delicate, impermanent works of genius that was determined to contain what was alive or soon would be.

Is there any doubt that the idea of a woven basket is an imitation of a woven nest, whose existence precedes basketry by no less than, say, one hundred and twenty-five million years, at the origin of nesting birds? We do not hesitate to elevate basketry to a folk art form. But bird nests? "The nest," we say, "is an expression of instinct," because that, we believe, differs from art, even the arts of folk, and places it in its proper relation to the supremacy of human forms, which are an expression of the self-conscious mind. We have ceased to see the nest as those long before us must have seen it: an amazing form of metaphorical and practical expression that is on the most intimate, accommodating terms with its immediate surroundings. An entirely other manner of being in a space.

One purpose of art is to reveal the beauty of forms by discovering order in daily chaos; or to put it more grandly: to discover the divine intention in what seems random. If baskets in fact do intimate the nest, perhaps then this form of art originates elsewhere than as an exclusively human impulse. What could be more a revelation of form discovered in chaos than a nest? Seeing shape and even purpose in otherwise randomly gathered materials, birds create no differently than we do, and perhaps they taught us how to conceive of the divine form embedded in the mundane. That assumption, if correct, is as cheerful as it is humbling. Unprovable as it is, I wish to believe, at the very least, that we learned to make this singular shape from others than ourselves, a stipulation that in no way diminishes the significance of our subsequent pursuits, the birds' initial inventiveness, nor our potential delight in either their work, our own, or, for that matter, the gods'.

For us, nest is always a four-letter word, one of the many profane, blunt, beautiful, drumbeat-like words native to Old English and its near relations. The origins of *nest* suggest our recognition of and respect for its genius. The Sanskrit root *nida* is related to nether—*ni-* meaning "down," "lower," "under." Thus, nest is associated with the darkness of earth, of soil, and from a certain flawed perspective, with what is impure and hellish. But if we permit a Blakean inversion (and I insist that we do), the nest is associated with the virtues of that netherworld: creativity, passion, generation, physical joy, warmth, sexual pleasure, nurturance. The *-da* of the Sanskrit is from the root *sed*, to sit: in the nest we interrupt our busy-ness, we sit down, as the Zen student may sit to meditate, choosing to be patient, present, calm, in the right place right now. My hurried snapshots are really incapable of revealing these virtues.

Even so, it is the nests of birds such as those in my snapshots that may spare us from our lonely, isolate selves. We, too, may learn to weave our own minds into the world; weave our minds of the stuff immediately at hand. Though he was meditating on the predicament of poets who live their lives in the provinces, far from the shining capitals of the world, Czeslaw Milosz may just as well have been speaking about anyone, even birds, even you or me, when he points to the creative intelligence of proximity to a familiar place and a particular knowledge of its myriad inhabitants: "A complete liberation from the gravitational force of the local and provincial condemns a poet to imitate foreign models." In another meditation, Milosz praises the stubborn greatness of a painter, condemned most of his life for being a foolish provincial, never straying far from his village, though in his village he was regarded with contempt. A failed painter who nevertheless insisted on the primacy of the local in his painting, who would later become: Cezanne. The local is one of the many paths to genius—and perhaps because of its anonymity and humbleness it is fraught with the most difficulty.

At a student art show, I recall stopping before a small pedestal in the gallery where a young artist had placed a nest she had woven from the cast-off stuff of her life—strips of pages torn from her journal, fabric from an old dress, white birch bark, dry ponderosa needles, and stalks of grass from her family's orchard. In this fine, porous, ephemeral bowl she placed fragments of blue eggs she had found. Who could fault even a clumsy, sophomore effort to make something so intimate? Like much else we might discover close at hand in the world, the nest points the way toward a knowledge of how we might choose to inhabit a place in that world and integrate our lives with that place. And, given the assumption that art derives from the gift of knowledge other species may have made to us about the near-at-hand presence of the divine, we are compelled to consider the dimensions of an older, prehistoric aesthetic, the genius of being fully alive in a place, which may require more than a snapshot, a passing glance.

The idea of a nest may in fact render our lives more complex and difficult, and therefore, perhaps, more meaningful.

❧❦

The nest does not intrude. Nor does it make claims of initial or exclusive rights. The nest blends in, vanishes into the landscape, and can only be discovered by serendipity, by surprise. Near my home in the Grande Ronde Valley, the great blue herons build large, haphazard piles of twigs in cottonwoods. The rookery I visit at the middle of the valley is a mile from the nearest road, and by the time the leaves open in the cottonwoods, the herons nested on their platforms high in the crowns of those trees have vanished entirely inside of green mist. Abandoned the remainder of the year, the rookery probably is not recognizable to anyone who does not know what he or she is looking for, or where even to look. At the local university there was a debate recently about changing the school mascot from a bearded, four-fingered mountaineer to the great blue heron. Most of those engaged in the debate did not know precisely what a blue heron is, great or not, nor where herons live, much less why anyone would want to name sports teams after them. Only a few joined the debate on the side of the heron, going so far as giving directions to the rookery at the middle of the valley, where herons have made a home along the river for the past ten thousand years. The deformed mountaineer—historically a recent interloper, but the source, evidently, of much personal identity, despite his missing digits—nevertheless remained the official mascot.

Soon after this debate exhausted itself, I canoed under the rookery; in a thirty-second-long exchange of glances, I looked up into the startled eyes of fifty pairs of herons who looked down into the eyes of an intruder. But I did not wish to intrude, rather to be permitted to vanish, to dispose of my threat (my unfortunate birthright) and live close by, as unobtrusively as any other bird.

The delight in discovering and remaining a moment in the presence of a nest is in the obviousness and paradoxical secretiveness of the nest, its joyful new life hidden close at hand.

Nests delighted the nineteenth-century English poet, John Clare, who wrote poems for virtually every bird nest he could identify by species. Clare is the master who tells us to open our eyes to the nests and grant them more than a glance. The obsessiveness of his particularity of vision belies his madness. His obsession may in fact have been a statement of the greatest lucidity of mind.

Unlike the newly enclosed and privatized rural English landscape that tormented Clare all his adult life, bird nests were a kind of subversive image of freedom and joy, where he "gleaned habitual love," in the presence of genuine life, removed, if only briefly, "From the vague world where pride and folly taunts." In the nest, Clare discovered the metaphor for habitation that he saw vanishing from human society, a metaphor that may seem as sentimental and precious to us as his "rustic" spelling and syntax. But for Clare the nest was as authentic and necessary as fresh bread. Of the pettichap's nest, he wrote:

> Had chance not lead us by it—may e'en now
> Had not the old bird heard us trampling bye
> And fluttered out—we had not seen it lie
> Brown as the road way side—small bits of hay
> Pluckt from the old propt-haystacks.

But once he saw what was hidden from him, Clare rejoiced in the particular facts of the nest:

> Withered leaves make up its outward walls
> That from the snub-oak dotterel yearly falls
> And in the old hedge bottom rot away
> Built like a oven with a little hole
> Hard to discover—that snug entrance wins
> Scarcely admitting e'en two fingers in
> And lined with feathers warm as silken stole
> And soft as seats of down for painless ease
> And full of eggs scarce bigger e'en then peas.

There are many examples in Clare's work—"The Wrynecks Nest," "The Yellow Wagtails Nest," "The Moorhens Nest," and so on— each compelling for its evocation of the genius of making that is animated by humility and a loyalty to the young. That such nests are vulnerable to deliberate or accidental intrusion goes without saying in a world where unconsciousness of and unconcern for lives other than our own is necessary to confirm the suspect values of suspect dominions. Thus, Clare's poems are full of the anxiety he hears in the songs of birds as they tend their nests.

For Clare, the nest, like the landscape itself, is an art form, "natures poesy," his true Master whose works he translates into poetry and prose to reveal the holiness of lives otherwise abused by ignorance or godless economic pragmatism. His hope was to preserve the idea of habitation that he saw disappearing from human communities. The "interior" domestic world of the nest insists on no distinct boundary between itself and the "exterior" landscape—it is a temporary form gleaned and shaped from that landscape, a natural part of that landscape, incongruous with anything other than that landscape. The nest thus belies the madness of Enclosure, the madness of boundaries we draw between ourselves and the rest of creation, rather than the madness of the poet, who lived the final twenty years of his life in the Northampton Asylum. Clare was probably the sanest man alive. Sane as the mind that makes a nest.

❧❧

One Saturday afternoon, my wife and I stood in the check-out line of the garden-supply department at Brainless-Mart. Customers dodged left and right as house sparrows in the rafters shat on their heads. Josefa and I stepped aside, out of the line of fire, though others insisted on remaining in the original line—a yellow stripe painted on the concrete, so they knew precisely where they were to stand at all times. We enjoyed watching this profane performance. The stubborn were shat upon again and again. "Damned birds!" someone muttered, jumping back. Damned indeed! The electric conduit passing along the underside of the corrugated metal roof provided a fine place for making nests, and given the sizeable amount of weeds and human trash endemic to Brainless-Marts nationwide and scattered along the asphalt and vacant lots, there was plenty of building material. Rags, rubber bands, newspaper. Poultry feathers, foil, shoe strings, shreds of Styrofoam and plastic cups. Dry stalks of salsify, bachelor buttons, and wild rye. "Couldn't they spray for these birds?" a disgruntled man asked no one in particular. And gray-white blobs splattered on his shoulder and at his feet.

Or consider the nest of the white-crowned sparrow, the house sparrow's much-studied country kin. She prefers open groves of trees and meadows among grasses and shrubs. While picking mushrooms last May, I wandered for hours in a kind of hallucinatory state, my attention drawn toward every insignificant shadow in the grass and forest slough. Once, bending to my knees to pick a morel, then another and another, I reached into the thick grass beside a nest, although I did not see the nest until the sparrow darted out, silent but for the nearly imperceptible flick of her wings as she fled. For a moment, I was uncertain if I had actually seen anything at all. But when I bent closer to the ground, and looked into the clump of sedge growing from a crevice in the outcrop of andecite, there was a fine little nest lined with her feathers and the shed white hair of deer and elk. Five tiny eggs, the size of jelly beans, creamy white and spotted red.

Another day: running along an abandoned logging road, I scared a wild turkey from her nest. It was she, however, who scared me witless, even before I was aware of the fright I had caused her. Not three feet away from where I passed, she tore off downhill, dragging her wings, and blurting, "Murder, murder!" When I composed myself, every follicle of hair on my body finally relaxing and lying flat again against my skin, I peered over the crumbling edge of the road. She had not woven but scratched out a nest in the flat accumulation of forest duff behind a stump on the steep hillside. Eight eggs, each as big as a child's fist. An hour later, she was back on her nest, her bronze and cream feathers blending into the mottled light of the forest floor. She appeared to be no more than a calm, flat oblong of barred light. Though when I looked closely, her eyes, bright obsidian beads, fixed on me from the shadows.

And again: waking from a nap on the grass along the Imnaha River, and looking up this time along a bluff of basalt, I saw an ouzel fly off across the water. Then an angry racket started up inside a globe of grass and twigs that miraculously adhered to sheer rock. Five tiny, orangish-yellow triangles shoving forward to the edge of the hole. Beaks opening and closing and squawking greedily. To get a closer look, I had to wade the river and climb the smooth-faced rock. A melding of love, hunger, and despair greeted the shadow I cast across the nest, which became suddenly a shadow they knew to fear. A stranger at the door. The nestlings hunkered back silently into the down of the nest, as I lost my grip and slid back down the riverbank. Soon the adult ouzel hurried back, a beak full of mayflies. A riot of relief erupted within the nest.

And yet another day, at a friend's homestead on the Middle Fork of the John Day River: as we talked under a canopy of hundred-year-old locust trees, two pairs of kingbirds busily wove nests from the shed winter coats of livestock in the nearby pastures. And, before departing, I stepped into the privacy under the dark, low-slung branches of a fir tree. As urine splashed at my feet, I glanced around in the cool gloom under the tree, and in the fork of a low limb, an astonishingly bright yellow and red tanager gaped at me in disbelief. He huddled in the privacy of the nest he and his mate had only half-completed in their hurry to fuck. I offered my apologies and stepped away.

❧❧

In the eleventh century Taoist painter Fan K'uan's great landscape painting of the area near Chang-an, *Travelers Among Mountains and Streams*, the central imagery is foregrounded by rocks, the forms of which are repeated three times in the composition of the painting. Our gaze rises rapidly from the rocky foreground to a rocky, forested middle ground, to the high mountain crags and their familiar ribbon of waterfall. Because the compositional strategy is such as to distract us from the human presence in this landscape, we fail, at least at first glance, to observe the mule drivers in the lower right corner, and temple above. Although this painting employs its own by now familiar Romantic tropes about the nature of human spirituality, the difference between Fan K'uan's vision of the proper scale of human presence in the landscape and, say, Casper David Frederick's well-known nineteenth-century painting *The Wanderer Above the Mists*, demonstrates a terrifying inflation of human self-importance in the latter. For Fan K'uan, the human road, the travelers, their domestic stock, and the temple are tiny, indistinct, and inconspicuous, vanishing into the landscape. In the more modern painting—a Romantic expression of human spiritual longing—a single individual, a Nietzschean superman, dominates an entire landscape, all of which is summoned to his feet. And why? Merely to reflect his personal spiritual elevation? It is an appalling image. Unironic and arrogant, it not only diminishes nature, it also denies the individual's more complex and humbling relations to nature. In the case of Frederick, the Egotistical Sublime arrives not at a vision of humility, suggesting the proper scale of human presence in landscape, but is precisely an expression of the rapacious mind that Clare—and the birds his work praised— most feared.

Fan K'uan sees absolutely nothing grandiose about human beings. We exist, but only as small, fragile, almost transparent presences (a few light brush strokes) below the numinous mountain cliffs. Our lives are as humble, vulnerable, and transient as a bird's nest. His depiction of the human presence in the landscape is aesthetically lovely exactly because he does not permit us to impose, but asks us to accommodate ourselves to the landscape. His human road does not cut through the rocks in the foreground as an interstate highway might, but detours around them. Nor are his spiritual longings expressed by anything remotely like a contemporary church surrounded by the acres of asphalt that are necessary to accommodate the congregation's SUVs. Rather, Fan K'uan paints a temple, the roofs of which are barely distinguishable from the crown of the pines that surround it— and that serve, it seems, as a model for its design. And the temple is small in comparison to the Creation itself, contingent entirely on that greater power to allow its continued presence on the steep pitch of the mountainside. And if what I mistake for a temple is actually a palace of the wealthy and powerful—all the better! It does not attempt to proclaim the pipsqueak majesty of its residents. Glance in its direction, and you may not even see it.

ℒℒ

The poet William Everson once wrote about an incident that occurred while he was interred as a CO during the Second World War. The artist Morris Graves visited the camp one day during the war. Graves "arrived unannounced, quietly locating at the mouth of Big Creek on the Oregon coast near Yachats, where we were stationed." Everson's work detail that day was assigned to clear a new trail and began haphazardly clearing brush. Graves, however, asked that everyone pause a moment and consider where the mountain might prefer the trail to be made.

> *"Please," he said, "before we begin we had best consult the spirit of this place.... Let us regard the underlying purpose.... Let us discover why things are as they are.... Observe the inclination of the slope, and above it the drift of the foliage. Do you sense the slight depression there where the leaves have drifted? It is the clue to the*

vector, the stress-line in the rock below. It is the flaw that enables us to enter into the presences here, and understand their disposition." Then, with supreme deliberation, the tact that comes only from an achieved authority, he reached in his arm and extracted a dead branch. "The trail begins here," he said simply.

Of course the mountain may have preferred that no trail be made, but the question of permission that Graves raised is the essential thing: understand the question and an answer becomes unnecessary. Asking the right question—in this case, asking permission—assumes a dialogue may exist between ourselves and the world we inhabit. Inquire of the landscape and we may then honor its permission to proceed by looking close at hand for the shapes of our habitation, and the necessary and sufficient materials to create those indigenous forms. If we try to make our own living space vanish into its native place, we practice the aesthetic of the bird's nest, which is always an accommodation to the landscape that demonstrates an awareness of the ingenious potential inherent in the local. The nest is an expression of the complexity of relations, of mutualities that develop between species and the landscapes they inhabit. John Clare's fascination with bird nests reflects a scale of knowing and intimate particularity that is always possible for human beings, while at the same time providing a metaphor of how we may choose to live generously among our neighbors. We are not absolutely isolated individuals, but live in a larger and more complexly defined community than that. Clare's was a vision of humility, like Graves', an acknowledgment that our place might yet be a modest, rather than dominate, one. And respecting the integrity of those lives no more or less privileged than our own, each of us equal to the other, we might choose to live less conspicuously in the landscape, developing the habits of mind that permit us to be simultaneously present and almost invisible.

A Rant

On a beer run twenty years ago with my friend Philip, a landscape architect, we were driving back up the mountain lane toward his party, when he pulled over suddenly to the side of the road and began to rhapsodize about an abandoned farmhouse in the meadow north of the road. It was one-story, just a few rooms, stuccoed and painted mint green, its windows broken out, doors shot up, slate shingles heaped in piles around the foundation like old drifts of snow the roof had shed after a winter storm.

Between us and the farmhouse was a line of tall, partly dead Lombardy poplars that shaded the south-facing house in summer. "Look at this. It's lovely," he said. "You know why? It's unobtrusive." I nodded, but Philip knew that I didn't see exactly what he saw. "It blends into the hillside," he said. "It can't be seen from below or above. It's out of the wind. Shaded in summer, protected in winter. Whoever built this had no desire to draw attention to himself. He paid a kind of respectful attention to what was around him."

All around us were early prototypes of what are now the ubiquitous "monster houses," "starter castles," "MacMansions," "castles in a box." These massive encumbrances on the landscape wallow in plain sight, demanding recognition of, and obsequiousness to, their owner's apparent power, wealth, and bad taste. Twenty years later, the abandoned farmhouse and its dying poplars are long gone. On that same Montana hillside in the Bitterroot Valley, above where it stood, is an English Tudor estate, what another acquaintance of mine called, looking at the Montana hillsides swarming with humongous houses, "An epidemic of Modern American Dentistry Design."

The brother-in-law of a close friend of mine is an architect (or calls himself one) who has grown rich designing monster houses in the Carolinas. The typical luxury development there, as elsewhere, surrounds the requisite golf course—"improved nature," as the brochures boast. The houses are unimaginably expensive; many are valued at millions of dollars. Often they are second homes, visited only briefly during the year. And these houses are vast, ten thousand square feet or more, though typically housing the average-sized American family of three and seven-tenths more or less human beings. These houses contain not just living quarters and dining areas, kitchens, pantries, servants' quarters, and as many as a dozen bathrooms (each wired for electronic services), but also gyms, theaters, lap pools, and libraries with authentic-looking books. One may live almost an entirely self-contained, secure, atomized existence, and seldom have to encounter anyone outside of the immediate family. Locked and guarded gates at the entry to the development protect the inhabitants from ever having to deal with (no doubt dangerously envious) creeps like me. Perhaps such people as those who live in these developments are being groomed for life in outer space. They would certainly be the most likely to be able to afford the journey. Slipping the "surly bonds of earth," as Ronald Reagan was fond of saying in his patriotic dotage. The only practical impediment to such interplanetary life would be how to satisfy the innate urge to golf.

⋛⋚

There is a subspecies of the monster house with grandiose designs on the landscape: its fetish is with distance, an uncluttered space that can nevertheless be framed by the architecture of the house. And nowhere is this more evident than in the western United States. Despite, or because of, the picture-postcard scenery framed by its many windows, the monster house of the American West is alienated from the landscape it supposedly celebrates. The picture window is the perfect symbol of its disconnection from the proximity of earth.

Several years ago, returning to a trailhead into the Weminuche Wilderness, which we had not visited in over a decade, my family and I passed a prodigious vacation home perched on a hilltop. Does it go without saying that a decade earlier this area of southwestern Colorado was largely a ranching community with a strong Spanish presence going back centuries, that has since been supplanted by golf courses and condominium developments for absentee owners? The particular monster house we drove past, how big was it? Ten, thirty, fifty thousand square feet? I can only guess. It seemed, however, the equivalent of a medium-sized warehouse. It was offensively big, even as it swelled with pipsqueak self-importance below the San Juans—mountains so stormy, weirdly contorted, ominous, in places so steep and high they forbid access. For the owners of this monster house, the mountains no doubt are a deeply inspirational Egotistical Sublime: the San Juans are framed by the house's architecture, or more accurately, the economic power of its owners whose superiority is reflected by the "majesty" they observe from their picture windows.

Sited on the crest of a hill, and visible from all directions, this particular monster was a log house, with three wings, constructed from old-growth ponderosa pines. The entire hilltop bulldozed and reshaped to reflect the architect's landscape "design"—the original site somehow having been judged inferior. A perimeter fence and two massive electronic gates—one at the county road and the other a quarter mile closer to the house—secured it from unscheduled visitors. The occupants of the monster house had no intention of ever subjecting themselves to the conditions of the wilderness their north-facing windows framed. Why bother to construct such opulence around one's self if one intends only to abandon it, even briefly, for a cramped wet tent in the forest? The golf course (formerly agricultural fields) was visible in the opposite direction from the mountains, and was a short drive from the five-bay garage that was larger by half than my own house in Oregon.

But the framing of nature in picture windows doesn't come without certain risks that only a tough, pioneering (and litigious) sensibility may meet along the trail and surmount. In Bend, Oregon, one neighbor recently sued another for intruding upon his picture-window views. Each litigant was wealthy enough, of course, to hire a passel of lawyers to defend, without a trace of self-irony, the exclusive rights to first intrusion. And each argued the classic delusion of white settlers in the American West: "I alone am the true Adam." The original Adam lived in an exotic garden, beyond the walls of which none of its life could likely survive, though he was intimate enough with its fruits to taste their knowledge and to name the animals with whom he shared that contained space. The sullen contemporary Adam regards nature as little more than an essential element for a window treatment, the necessary scenery to maintain, or much better yet, to boost property values. But scenery, as always, is a fabulous lie. There is a bulldozer, literal or metaphorical, cropped from the frame. And any intrusion upon that illusion of inviolate scenery is cause for a quarrel.

ℒℒ

One night in the Bass Creek Campground in the Bitterroot Mountains, the campground already full, a young man pulled up next to us and asked if he could pitch his tent near ours. We agreed, and soon we were sharing a beer and stories. He was a carpenter from Aspen, Colorado, and for the past four years had been helping to build a fifty-five-thousand-square-foot vacation home for an Arab sheik. The sheik wished to visit briefly during the Christmas holidays, but the interior finish work had not yet been done, as the materials were rare and the work intricate. It was going to take another year or more to complete once the materials arrived from abroad. The sheik, however, was undaunted, and told the contractor to finish the work, sparing no expense. And so, using high-quality but locally available materials, the crew completed the work—right down to the flooring, carpets, tiles, fixtures, and moldings. The sheik arrived, partied and skied for two days, and left, ordering the contractor to tear out all the work he and his crew had done for the visit and complete the job when the proper materials arrived. That is exactly what they did, tearing out all the carpets, flooring, tiles, fixtures, and moldings, salvaging for themselves what they could, and hauling the remainder to the dump.

I know, I know, that carpenter should have been grateful for the work.

ℒℒ

In a canyon above the town where I live, the wealthy scion of a wealthier father (an argument for higher estate taxes if ever there was one) has begun buying up parcels of ranch land where many of the citizens of the town below had walked in what once was treated as a commons, and where in the winter I many times stumbled upon huge herds of elk.

But the wealthy scion has built: first, a modest cabin (for the caretaker), next a large sheet-metal horse barn, a "hunting cabin," a ten-thousand-square-foot "summer home" (for his three-person family), and a massive covered riding arena visible from five miles away. The contractor who has built all of these structures, not without (I hoped) a measure of sad irony as he dug up old Nez Perce root-gathering camps in the process, has begun to take on the airs of his lord to whom he is now (apparently) a loyal retainer. We met along a stretch of county road that bisects the wealthy scion's property and that the wealthy scion has tried to have vacated by the county. The contractor had gone horseback riding across the "ranch" the weekend before, he told me, with the owner and "their friends," and never saw any elk, much less sign of elk. Imagine that! I wonder where they have gone? One winter day three years ago, I found a herd of two hundred and fifty elk, resting in the pines at precisely the place the wealthy scion has built his summer home, whose windows provide a lordly view indeed of the valley below, of town, and the mountains that surround it.

The contractor had ridden along the Oregon Trail, which bisects the scion's property for approximately ten miles.

"Remember," I said, "there was a man used to walk that trail every year on his birthday."

"Oh, yeah," the contractor nodded, recalling our now vanquished elder, "the old barber downtown."

"He walked that route every year until he was ninety-six years old," I said. He was quite a presence in the community. The old man walked (vigorously) everywhere, with a soiled blue rucksack on his straight back. He'd repaired that rucksack a few times, replacing the shoulder straps and waistband with ropes. His ten-mile hike across the Blue Mountains along the Oregon Trail was an act of pilgrimage to honor his parents' and grandparents' generations.

Whatever the historical facts that complicate our conventional myth of the Oregon Trail, that old man's pilgrimage at least affirmed the egalitarian values of America's promise to ordinary men and women, and connected those of us who witnessed it with the lives of people who would otherwise seem distant and abstract. That those values are partly founded on savagery toward the actual possessors of the land, of course, is the complication our myth denies. But all that is now beside the point, isn't it?

Access to that historic trail is forbidden by the new landowner, who has posted the land with threats of litigation against trespassers. The only potential trespassers I can think of are his neighbors who live in the community year round.

Years before the appearance of our wealthy scion, a rancher rented the same property one summer and fall to graze his cattle. He posted the property with signs that read:

No Trespassing.
(Survivors Will Be Prosecuted.)

Very funny. Of course, I ignored these signs and walked wherever I damn well pleased. And it was a good thing, too. One morning as I was returning in my car down the canyon, having walked on the ridges above town that the renter had posted, I came across a pickup truck and horse trailer overturned in a gully beside the road. The driver had lost traction on the ice, slipped off the road and flipped the trailer. There were horses inside. Hysterical horses. I jumped out and together with that scared, shaken rancher, removed the horses from the trailer, tried to calm them down, tied them up and drove the renter back to town, where we went searching for a wrecker to pull him out of the gully. Once I realized who he was, I asked him about the No Trespassing signs, and pointed out that had I obeyed his wishes, I wouldn't have come along that morning, and he and his horses could have been in a lot worse shape.

"Yeah," he said. "I didn't mean nothing by those signs anyway." I recall that the man had a very difficult time finding anyone willing to help him pull his truck and trailer out of the gully.

But the wealthy scion, I'm afraid, does mean something by his signs. Letters forbidding anyone to cross his land have been mailed by his lawyer to his neighbors who had "permission" to walk on the private land: "the walking agreements are, as of today—September 20, 2000—being revoked."

"I wonder," I said to the contractor the other day, "if the old barber would be given permission now to make his pilgrimage?"

The contractor saw the critical direction my question was leading. "Don't know," he said, and ended the conversation, with a world-weary sigh. "Guess I'll have to head down to the village now for lunch." He put his pick-up in drive and did.

The village? Of course. That is the ultimate meaning of the monsters who have filled up the country with their conspicuously ugly manors. They are the new feudal lords on whose property we have become, if not serfs or slaves, then trespassers, poachers, irritants, pests, vermin. Call us what you like, lords of this world, I for one will not bow down.

Healing In

K nown prior to white settlement as Kup-Kup-pa or "Place of the Cottonwoods," the Grande Ronde Valley, where I live, was a commons. It was never disputed territory among area tribes—Nez Perce and Cayuse shared its resources in season with the Walla Walla and Umatilla, all of whom made periodic visits to fish for salmon, gather camas, and hunt for large game. No tribe ever made an exclusive claim to the Grande Ronde Valley. In 1827, Peter Skene Ogden, a white fur trapper, seeing how the Cayuse conserved the resources here, particularly the beaver—whose pond building served then as now to create greater river complexity, increasing the diversity of species, and likewise the overall health of the valley— wrote in his journal: "If the Cayuse will not ruin the beaver in their own lands we must for them." The violence of Ogden's desire was perverse, and today is so pervasive and ongoing that we have few places left locally to witness an alternative way of defining our relations to the valley, surrounding foothills, and mountains. We are condemned, it seems, only to enact violence. One hundred and seventy years of mining, logging, and agriculture have left the river and its tributaries empty of both water and salmon, the foothills and mountains plundered, stripped of trees, and eroding.

The small town I live in on the western edge of the Grande Ronde Valley is bounded by the Blue Mountains. To the north rises the six-thousand-foot profile of Mount Emily, its forests crisscrossed by logging roads and washed-out motorcycle trails, along which some residents of town dump garbage. In the last week alone I have found garden and lawn debris, a dried-out Christmas tree, and the corpse of the family dog tossed on top. To the south is Glass Hill, the roads on which are also used as a dump. On Glass Hill, however, the forests have been removed by a local timber conglomerate. One dismayed timber executive let slip in my presence, "The land up there looks nuked." A revealing choice of words. To "nuke" our enemies, we must hate them with such an all-consuming hatred as to be willing to kill or horribly sicken everyone and everything and render their place of habitation unfit for healthy life. Local logging practices have enacted this pure hatred of nearby forests in much the same spirit as Peter Ogden perceived beaver pelts. It is ironic, however, that we became our own enemy in this case, impoverishing the landscape and making it less inhabitable for ourselves.

These areas adjacent to town, however assaulted by human desires, create an abrupt edge to urban development in the valley. And though these hills are zoned as secondary agricultural or timber lands, and are grazed part of the year by ubiquitous herds of beef cattle, the land, despite its heavy industrial and recreational uses, is inhabited by wild animals.

Principal among the mammals (or the most attractive and obvious) are herds of Rocky Mountain elk, smaller populations of mule deer, and a handful of whitetail deer, who thrive in cut-over land and whose presence suggests that the forest landscape here is fragmented. There are also occasional bobcats and bears, a single ghostly lynx, coyotes, and not a few cougars, one of whom strolled through the hospital parking lot on a recent Friday afternoon. Throughout the warmer months of the year, until drought or famine begins to drive them back into the valley, these animals live in the islands of forest and meadow that remain in these foothills and mountains. It is common to see these animals in town in winter. Yesterday's police blotter in the newspaper reports that an officer responded to a "barking dog complaint on C Avenue." The officer found a "fairly large herd of elk" grazing in the backyards on the block. Deer browse along city streets at night, too, stalked by cougars who may take a break from the hunt to curl up on my neighbor's front porch. Coyotes sometimes will break into weird chorus at a street-corner congress late at night. Having feasted on windfall in the overgrown orchards, and full of fermented, overripe fruit, bears fall asleep in the tall weeds of a dead-end street, where on occasion, we have startled them awake in autumn, their bewildered faces covered in an icy rime.

But the presence of these wild animals is not exotic really, nor does it simply provide the basis for rustic stories to impress or appall visitors from urban areas where the edge between the domestic and the wild has vanished under commercial and suburban sprawl. These large mammals, among many shyer and more scarce others, share with us the edge of an old wound.

ℒℒ

During winter, below Glass Hill, in wild orchards just off Foothills Road, dozens of finches, chickadees, and juncos will scatter when I step into the frozen lane. They dodge through scrub thickets of hawthorn and wild roses, scolding my interruption of their foraged feast. They are cross with me even as I offer fists full of sunflower and millet, seeds bouncing on stiff mud at my feet. If it is Sunday morning, iron bells ring miles away, announcing the persistent wound of the Sixth Day of Creation, when we emerged, shaped from the same mother-mud of the animals' earlier world. That world before our arrival was not yet betrayed by our misguided belief in our dominion—an absurd, self-justifying hierarchy in which we place ourselves closer to God than all others. Only the world prior to the Sixth Day was a world without irony and without end.

Still, wild animals persist at the edge of this wound, and seem reluctant to abandon us entirely to ourselves or our God, as they are unwilling to abandon their former habitats, onto which the local urban landscape has encroached. Riparian areas disappear, followed by an increase in downstream flooding. Local creeks are forced underground, into culverts, further increasing the risk of flood elsewhere. Ornamentals have replaced native shrubs and forbs, forcing native species to the steep, "unbuildable" edges of town, where they thrive despite the drought that kills the exotic plants. A grid of streets is now built over springs and seeps that once were reached only by game trails. The basements of houses on the Spring Street Hill, on which I live, fill with this water animals once bowed to drink, sump pumps humming now, discharging the excess water into sewers. Our encroachment, though, brings a violence into the landscape simply because it ignores the possibility of dialogue, imposing instead our disastrous will, the conditions of our supposed dominion dictated to all other beings who wish to live here as well.

The violence in us corrupts all our relations with the landscape and its other inhabitants. We assure that Peter Ogden's perversion defines us. There is, Robert Adams, says, "[a] widespread nihilism that now extends throughout much of the population. Witness the reflexive littering, the use of spray paint on rocks, the girdling of trees . . ., the use of off-road vehicles to maximize the violence of their impact." This, sadly, extends beyond the physical geography of the landscape and includes our relations with other inhabitants. Remember the hundreds (thousands!) of animals, large or small, that each of us pass on the highway each year, killed and left to be humiliated, pulverized by the speed of our going elsewhere.

Only we are deceived by the clarion bells of Sunday mornings.

The church bells are the echo of our loud retreat from dialogue, from a negotiated place of habitation. We've turned away and denied the implications of that returned, potentially erotic gaze of the world. The wound originates in the moment we divert our eyes. John Berger points out that the returned gaze of animals, if recognized, for example, would complicate our relations with them, and suggest their own mysterious inwardness and intelligence. Recognition implies the possibility, if not the necessity, for dialogue. We deny their gaze exists. The animal may only be the object of our interest, but never the reverse: "In the accompanying ideology, animals are always the observed. The fact that they can observe us has lost all significance. They are the objects of our ever-extending knowledge. What we know about them is an index of our power." What if an animal insists that we look into its eyes? We project our violence outward then, arguing that our presence in the landscape is "civilizing" and that everything else is animated by its own instinctual violence, from which we must be kept safe. What if an animal, especially a predator, living at the margins of the city returns our gaze? In short: kill the beast.

℘℘

Last week, the six-year-old black bear Josefa and I have encountered on nearby game trails in the foothills—finding where he slept the night; seeing the yellow-jacket nests he had raided; the rotted logs he had overturned to eat the ants; rocks he had moved to devour swarms of ladybugs; his fresh piles of mountain ash-, apple-, rosehip-, or plum-pit-laden shit; or simply finding his large rain-filled tracks in the mud on an autumn day—when this bear was discovered once too often asleep in a tree in a suburban backyard of people who it seems evident possess a greater right than he to occupy the forested west hills of town, this bear was shot dead.

Another local example of this conflict between people and animals is the booming population of cougars, who, until a citizen initiative outlawed their being hunted by hounds, kept their distance from human beings. Although biologists are not yet certain, it appears that, with the hunting pressure removed, cougars have lost their aversion to people. In addition, their numbers have benefited from the cyclically larger numbers of game on which to prey. "Game" being the object of the hunter's desire, the need to decimate predators, therefore, is the single idea our state representative, an avid hunter, possesses in response to his "concerns" about the increase in cougar "incidents." His wife, he claims, has been stalked by a cougar. Therefore, he proposes a "special hunt" to remove six hundred cougars (and bears) from the nearby forests, a number that probably well exceeds the total.

There is some possible negotiation between us and the cougars that is not occurring because cougars are, from a peculiar perspective, "useless" (even if you hunt them for trophies) because unlike bear you cannot eat them. As one hunter said to me, "You know cats: clean on the outside, filthy on the inside." Hunting them without dogs is impossible unless one is a particularly fit and gifted hunter, and most hunters are not. Hence, cougars play the ironic role of a foil, a mirror in which our diminished physical capacities are made clear.

And because cougars are "useless," they really have no reason to exist, but because they exist they are interfering with sport that hunters could have to attain the same end: keeping wild ungulant populations in "balance," to use the popular cliché. Local citizens prefer the security of being alone at the top of the food chain.

As I write this, a wolf who "strayed" into Oregon last winter, and who was captured and returned to the Selway-Bitterroot Wilderness on the Idaho-Montana border, is perhaps on her way back to Oregon, where she will again generate rancorous debate about her presence here and her impact on cattle and sheep production. Already, the nearby Wallowa County Court, prescient as ever, has banned wolves from returning to the county. In central Idaho, grizzly bears may soon be reintroduced (or may find their own way back). No doubt, too, they will eventually make the Oregon trip as well, and will, again, generate angry debate about whether or not it is "appropriate" for them to live here in what was their former native range. What is missing in our discussions of these reappearances of large and potentially dangerous predators is the common sense middle-ground of negotiated space. Because we can only imagine ourselves relating to these creatures violently if they return (and possibly return our gaze), we insure a continuation of cultural violence. Our debate will be ugly. And our behavior toward these animals will be even uglier. It will be cruel.

There is a Coeur d'Alene story about the time before the wound infected the negotiable space we must share with others. During huckleberry season, when people were gathering berries that were as valuable to them as to the grizzly bears, bears and people nevertheless managed to get along. "We'll pick these over here, and if you Bear People don't mind, you can pick those over there. Is that OK?" Evidently it was, as people and bears went about their necessary and "useful" activities side-by-side, without conflict, because they could still talk to each other. Our problem today is that cougars, wolves, and bears seem angry at us for our unwillingness to talk it over. Apparently they do not like being ignored or treated as though they are (or should be) invisible. Nor do they approve of being murdered any more than, say, young African American or Hispanic men approve of being hunted by the police in our cities for the sole reason that their returned (and often hostile) gaze complicates the ease we otherwise feel, complicit as we are with the ludicrous racial dominion that is one of the corrupt foundations of the nation.

The bear, wakened from his sleep and shot last week, was reported to be "dangerously agitated." I'll bet.

&2&

One autumn an elk hunter on Glass Hill came across a cougar. He explained later, "It looked like it might at any moment attack me." So he shot the cougar through the forehead. It is unwise to second-guess this incident—who knows how any of us would act when confronted by such a potentially dangerous situation?—but I doubt the hunter was in any danger. Cougars do not typically attack grown men. From discussions with a man who had been stalked and attacked, it is clear that he did not have any time to really think about whether or not he was in any danger; the cougar was already in mid-pounce when he raised his rifle and literally pushed the barrel into the cougar's mouth, as though it were a spear. "I never even had time to consider if the safety was on or off. As it turned out, it was off." The man on Glass Hill shot the cougar at a still-safe distance of thirty yards. The cougar was not charging; it only appeared to the hunter that there was a possibility that it might charge. I saw the animal in the back of a Fish and Wildlife officer's pickup. It was a large and powerful creature, weighing one hundred and fifty pounds, tawny colored, with foot pads and claws the size of human hands, intimidatingly powerful thighs and shoulders, and an improbably thick long tail. Its incisors were an inch and a half long, made all the more frightening by the massive jaw and muscles that ran upward toward the temples of the face, powerful enough to break a deer's or elk's or human being's neck. Awesome as the animal seemed even dead, the real cause of the cougar's death was not its aggressiveness but the hunter's fear, and the opportunity that fear had for expression in the singular fact of his high-powered rifle.

I have walked in that forest many times and seen elk and deer, though I have only twice seen other people. Once in winter, I crossed the tracks of a mountain lion—possibly the dead one. Though I am well aware that I may one day meet a lion on the trail, and that the outcome will be unpredictable, I have seldom felt so uneasy in the forest as in the presence of the two eager hunters recently encountered on Glass Hill, who unshouldered their rifles and took blind aim when they heard me approaching along the trail.

Another time I entered a meadow, just off a logging road, where a young pine had grown up alone. The tree was no more than twelve inches in circumference. Ten steps from the tree, scattered among clumps of bunchgrass, lay hundreds of empty shotgun shells. The ponderosa had been toppled by buckshot aimed again and again at a spot on the trunk about chest high. The only irony in this ugly scene was that the tree had fallen across the spot where the gunman (or men) stood. A teenage prank born of boredom and aimlessness, perhaps. But I can't shake the feeling of dread such scenes evoke. All living things must endure the threat such actions imply. It is like the latent threat of rape that pervades social relations and that women must endure as a fact of their birth. Every autumn, I come upon mutilated game animals shot for the sheer "pleasure of killing" that I often hear unself-consciously described by some hunters. There is a quality of cowardice and psychological darkness in such acts of violence, an unwillingness on the part of those involved to resist their apparent delight in aggressive power, their dominion over others, their power to command the life or death or humiliation of another living being.

Our relation to what is wild or autonomous in nature is corrupt, reactionary, adolescent. We act as though the forests are the weird Nietzchean paradise in which we express our "pure spirit," testing its mettle against nature: "less secure, less stable, less firmly anchored than any other animal; [man] is the sick animal." At best ours is a sentimental response to a change that occurred long ago in our relations to the world that sustains us, when we began to imagine ourselves free and separate from its dominion over us. And this assumes, here in the American West, that at some vague point in the past, the western landscape was one vast, trackless wilderness, where a man (of course) was strangely free to live without self-discipline or obligation to any other living thing. Individual autonomy is the chief value of our social relations. Which is complete hogwash.

At a public hearing on water quality in our watershed, the man leading the discussion cancelled the next meeting because, he explained, he would be "up in the wilderness at elk camp." This fifty-year-old farmer then deconstructed right before our eyes, and like an adolescent boy told everyone in the room he intended either "to get me an elk or get real drunk for two weeks, whichever comes first, and hopefully both." Elk camp is a local code word for the opportunity of men (in virtually all cases) to celebrate an annual bacchanal. In their wake, the forest is strewn with feces, garbage, beer cans, broken bottles, and animal parts. One group of hunters from Portland was arrested for game violations this past year in an elk camp that was surrounded by weeks of garbage they had just tossed into the forest around them. Unprocessed game, evidently shot for no reason other than the "pleasure" of doing so, lay rotting on the ground throughout the camp. I recently discovered another elk camp where hunters had taken along a large Wylie Coyote doll (yes), opened a slit in the crotch of the doll, and shoved beer bottles between its legs for target practice, after which they threw the doll into the smoldering ashes of their fire.

☙☙

The most civilizing force in our otherwise savage local culture could be the redefinition of what is wild. Let us quiet the brutality and savagery in ourselves by permitting a newly recognized wild a more prominent presence in our daily lives. We need to ask ourselves, for example, where is the appropriate place to observe and be observed by wild animals or wild nature—in increasingly fragmented and isolated islands of official wilderness? Or the abused "marginal" lands just above town? Or is it possible to incorporate wild presences within the boundaries of our "made" landscapes?

Certainly the separation of landscapes—urban, suburban, rural, wild—is not resulting in healthier, intact, or liveable spaces. In the local wilderness area, for example, camp fires will be banned above seven thousand feet this summer, and camping near lakes is being further restricted as backpackers and horsepackers continue to destroy the "protected" wild landscape. "Wildness" of the sort wilderness areas supposedly protect is a farce. Even "wild" landscapes are managed and cultivated, though on a scale that dwarfs the domestic kitchen garden. What is "wild" is something far more fundamental and that exists equally in all these landscapes.

Nor does incorporating "wildness" into an urban landscape mean the privilege of witnessing "majestic" animals on our city streets (although I like this disquieting dissonance a great deal), but seeing the natural processes that are perpetually trying to heal the wound of the Sixth Day as the ultimately wild presence in our lives. I remember as a child, working in my family's business, deep in the industrial brownfields of my hometown, where the soil that had not been covered by asphalt, bricks, or concrete was several inches thick with a mat of sun-baked, tar-like grease and cinders. Despite this, there was a tree that grew like a weed from every crack in the ground, that formed thickets and shaded the entire area surrounding the railyards where I worked in summer. It is not a native tree, the *Ailanthus altissima*, but it thrives in such extreme conditions, growing as much as eight feet a year. What could be wilder than this tree's desire to live, to recover such a human wasteland? It was only years later, as an adult, that I learned its common name: Tree-of-Heaven.

Rejuvenation, healing, forgiveness—essential to the ongoing health of any domestic household as to wild nature—should be observed, honored, learned from, and seen as an ethical model for human behavior. These processes offer an image of human habitation that heals into a place, that recognizes cultivation, the garden, the household, as being the best hope we have for living with a generous and healthy regard for others. What the domestic kitchen garden teaches us about wildness is far better than our longing to identify and visit ever more fragmented, isolated, "virgin" territories. The earth is full to bursting with people and the wish to find "uninhabited" wildlands is ludicrous, if not downright misguided. Rather than pick at it, it is time we begin to allow the wound to heal. This requires dialogue with what is nearest at hand.

In *The Desert Smells Like Rain*, Gary Paul Nabhan tells a story of two Papago Indian oases, A'al Waipia and Ki:towak, in the Sonoran Desert of Arizona. The older, A'al Waipia, was populated by people "since man came into the area" until 1957, when the U.S. Park Service removed the Papago to "preserve" the land as a bird sanctuary. The Papago had so healed into that place in the desert, they had created a habitat not only for their own form of ancient agricultural practice, but an extraordinary habitat for birds—common resident birds and rarer tropical species seldom or never seen that far north. The Papago were removed to an undeveloped oasis, Ki:towak, where they began to create a similar habitat to that of their former home. Soon, the birds began to disappear from the "bird sanctuary," and show up at the newly settled oasis. One Papago farmer explained it this way: "When people live and work in a place, and plant their seeds and water their trees, the birds go live with them. They like those places, there's plenty to eat and that's when we are friends to them." Nabhan speculates on the symbiotic relations between the human and nonhuman, and provides us with a clear metaphor for how our own forms of habitation and work may heal into places: "although [the Papago] didn't keep these [oases] as pristine wilderness—an Anglo-American expectation of parks in the West—the Papago may have increased their biological diversity." Such diversity is possible only if we are willing to listen to a multiplicity of voices. Diversity and its consequent health, too, suggest that some kind of dialogue exists between human beings and the other inhabitants of these garden-like oases. Looking at the abandoned A'al Waipia, Remedio, the Papago farmer quoted above, said of the untended and dying trees, "Poor things, such old trees left with no one to help them!"

The trees, no different than any other living things, remain vulnerable until we heal the self-inflicted wound that Peter Ogden suffered from and spread like a virus throughout this valley. Kup-kup-pa, The Place of the Cottonwoods. Where there are no longer great galleries of cottonwoods lining the flood plain. Where two centuries of greedy exploitation has spread its infection throughout the entire valley. Two centuries of heroic individualism run amok. Will we ever choose to healed into this place? How much more impoverishment can we bear?

Notes on the Erotic Life
of the Household

What am I to make of the Wildlife Art Show now at the Nightengale Gallery, mounted in conjunction with a conference of wildlife biologists? It is an improbable gathering of artworks. That the art is terrible goes without saying. One could just dismiss it as bad art and exit the gallery. But I find myself, drawn in, fascinated. What is odd is that the intended audience for this show (wildlife biologists) possesses perhaps the most detailed and intimate knowledge of the animals depicted here, and yet the images of these animals are pure Romantic fantasy. What could all of these Romantic images mean? The artists have ceased to see animals as they are, and instead imbued them with a moribund symbolism that has less to do with genuine animals and more to do with our disappointment in reality.

The paintings (they are all oils on canvas) possess the pictorial characteristics of a photograph. Their technique is conventional; that is, they are nominally realistic. Though the settings, the poses are as unrealistic as the likelihood that animals would pose. The predominate images are of antlered elk and deer standing above us, on majestic rocky ridges, and judging from the flora and geology, well above tree line, where it is more likely that we would see mountain goats or bighorn sheep. When we encounter a noble-looking bighorn sheep in these paintings, it is mature, of course, with an enormous curl of horns. A trophy. Last winter all the local bighorns unfortunately died of disease introduced by domestic livestock. The next most common image is of streams full of leaping salmon—an endangered species that has not "choked" streams such as those in the paintings for decades. And finally, there are images of nonplussed bears or cougars seen in stoic close-up. The last Legislature, however, attempted to pass a law demanding that six hundred cougars and bears be shot in our area (all of them) because of the perception that their predation interferes with ranching and recreational hunting. Thus, these paintings show us a fantasy about our actual relations to these animals. These paintings are a gathering of delusions. No, these paintings are worse than that: they are a hideous form of nostalgia, a form of mental illness.

ℒℒ

I saw a deer the other day. It was on a city street, grazing on ornamental shrubs. I saw an elk a few days before, resting under a tree in the mountains, surrounded by grazing Hereford cattle. And I have seen bear-sign, too, recently, up close: bucketfuls of black shit and rotted stumps torn apart. The last actual bear I saw was a mile away across a side canyon on the upper Umatilla River, a little black dot in a patch of yellow balsamroot. And my son saw a cougar yesterday: something large and very swift, with a long tail, leaping into the underbrush. In large part that is what a cougar is: a tail, vanishing. On a run two weeks ago I found a fawn's hindquarters without sign of rigor mortis, a recent cougar kill. The cougar, which I did not see, was no doubt very close by and did see me, as I struck what must have seemed to her an odd pose. A snake, too, is usually encountered in this oblique "pose": fleeing.

It is not these animals, though, that we usually encounter; these are not the animals with whom we are most acquainted. What about grey squirrels, field mice, packrats, voles, and shrews, to name just a few rodents that are so common in our daily lives we have created an entire industry to exterminate them? Forget eagles! What about lowly robins, house sparrows, ruby finches? What about the western toad? Bats? What about worms and slugs? And why not include insects as wildlife: flies, mosquitoes, bald-faced hornets, yellow jackets, bumblebees, ants . . . . Got your can of Raid? Your electronic patio-pest zapper? No romantic feelings for the wildlife with whom you are most familiar? We reserve our erotic emotions only for what is rare in our lives, and even then, we must lie about it, projecting instead an idealized image of our affections. We are like the teenage boy who falls in love with an ordinary girl who can never fulfill his desires, yet she must bear the weight and unreality of his projected idealization.

What is the truth about those "sexier" species, those sometimes cuddly-seeming creatures, or even other less anthropomorphic ones, about whom we nevertheless feel a sort of earnest goodwill? All of them possess (we like to tell ourselves) the purest form of freedom. Wildness, we call it, and are especially eager to admire it on the walls of the gallery. One of my students, a biology major, spent a recent summer stapling barcodes to the bellies of hatchery salmon. What a shock it is, when one encounters those large "sexy" mammals with radio collars around their necks. The fact is, such wildlife is "managed," is little more than a product provided for the sole use of hunters, the national forests and "wildernesses" being huge game parks for the exclusive use of men with rifles. The writer Jack Turner goes even further: he likens our management of wildlife to a concentration camp, the animals being the inmates—many of them are numbered, some with barcodes! That is a little extreme, but I see his point, and the biologists I have spoken with about this did not disagree with his characterization of their work.

But kill one of these imaginary, sexy animals and by a form of sympathetic transference you will possess its spirit of instinctual wiliness, strength, freedom. Or if blood sport is not for you, a wildlife painting (a virtual trophy) is a fine substitute. Either way, you take a place in an erotic fantasy of wildness.

❧ ❧

Elk season is now in full florid force. The "tourist" urban hunters are arriving in droves, many of them in massive RVs, towing jeeps and ATVs—hundreds of thousands of dollars spent to hunt elk one week a year. The tourist hunters stop in the grocery store and are hilarious to watch. Clearly, "back home" they do not shop for food, for they are hopelessly lost in the aisles of the store. They buy a lot of steak, and loaves of white bread to mop up the fat. The liquor store is doing a lively business. Many of these men are grossly overweight and unfit. How many will die of heart attacks this year in the forest? How many will need rescue? They seldom go in the forest, except now, and can only manage this with motorized vehicles. That most of them cannot shoot straight is borne out by the obscene amount of ammunition they take with them. It is all grotesque. It is the reason I have not hunted since leaving Montana, where the business of "canned" hunting—the ultimate, degraded fantasy, in which an animal is in a confined area and then stalked in a "guided hunt"—is now popular.

On the other hand, my friend Bruce "got his elk," as we say, without a great deal of fanfare, much less drunkenness. He took off half a day from work. Drove up to the watershed long before dawn. Parked and then hiked into the watershed, alone, with only two 30.06 shells. He would take one good shot or no shot at all. Within an hour, he found a young spike, stalked it briefly, positioned himself for what he hoped would be an opportunity to take that one good shot, then waited. He did not wait long. He killed the elk with one shot—which is another way of saying that he demands a premium of excellence and compassion from himself. He field dressed and quartered the animal, and was back at work by early afternoon. The end of hunting season.

For Bruce, the hunt is an adjunct of the domestic world, not a rejection of it. The hunt is no different, say, than harvesting and preserving the fruit from his orchard; growing garlic, scallions, or onions for the coming year; putting up four bins of potatoes. The elk equals his family's yearly supply of red meat. Hunting, ideally, is no different than gardening or gathering, though it is far more serious because we are killing a sentient being in whose eyes we recognize a familiar gaze, our own gaze returned. Hunting, like gathering, serves the household.

The "problem" of hunting is very simply the problem of its ethics, which begin, really, not in hunter training but in the domestic world. Or more precisely, the problem lies in the separation between the domestic world and the world of the forest and hunt. To close that distance, we need to ask how far can we extend, rather than exclude, familial love. As far as the forest? As far as the hunt? To the prey? To language?

ᘓᘓ

The first thing I saw as the new year began at the solstice was a herd of one hundred elk on Glass Hill. I had just been complaining to myself about how, after having lived in the midst of one of the largest elk herds in North America for six years, I had seen only a few solitary elk scattered in the forest. Then a herd ran past me at a distance of fifty yards in a column four and five abreast, and three hundred yards long. I counted only one mature bull elk among them—a six point. Many spikes. Many, many cows. The majority were yearlings and calves. Some of the older animals were nearly white.

I stood there up to my hips in snow, watching them pass for several minutes. Later, walking home, I recalled an Inuit black-pencil drawing of a hunter with his arms raised high in the air, a broad smile on his face, his teeth showing through his beard. The notes explain that he curved his arms inward above his head to imitate antlers, and, possibly, he is rotating his body as he makes this gesture, to signal his companions what he has just seen. Perhaps his bare hands signify the number of caribou. The title of the drawing, "Joyfully I See Ten Caribou" is therefore redundant.

It is the tone of joyfulness, conveyed either by image or by word, that is the source of the pleasure found within this drawing. Joyfulness, however, with its suggestion of the spontaneous demonstration of pleasure, is not a word I often associate with hunters in northeastern Oregon. Part of this Inuit hunter's pleasure originates in his identifying with the animal he is hunting. His gesture is a ritual of transformation, of the hunter becoming his prey. Living in an economy where surpluses are the most fragile and uncertain of possibilities accounts for a good deal of the hunter's joy. It is quite the opposite of the hunting practices I witness near my home during hunting season, where the brutal humiliation of the prey is common. Garbage bags full of the heads, hides, and entrails often are thrown out of moving vehicles, landing in grotesque splattered heaps in the ditches that line the roads. Sometimes, hunters even torment the corpse: last fall I came upon the remains of a deer whose head had been placed at the middle of an intersection of three forest roads, and repeatedly driven over, pulverized into the dust.

In an essay, in part, on the hunting practices of his grandfather, Robert Stubblefield has written about the cruelty of hunters who disrespect their prey. Their brutality, he says, is the result "of coldness, carelessness, or just a nameless malice inhabiting the void when other feelings dissipate." Whatever the motivation for such disgraceful behavior, whatever the rage born of inadequacy and fear, the relationship between hunter and prey is degraded, "with little or nothing exchanged." Joyfulness testifies to a full range of human emotions. Not the least of which are the imitation of and gratitude for the life one is about to take.

Joyfully I see two hundred elk running away!

ᗝᔓ

Having discovered what has remained elusive, I return each day in the hope of witnessing again the abundance of the Glass Hill herd. Instead, I spend most of my time inspecting signs of their having passed through. Their absence becomes my subject. I track them up to the orchards and follow their trail east along what I assume is their trail from the night before. Tracing the trail in reverse, up the hill into the timber, I find dozens of their beds pressed in the snow. Here is where they slept out of the wind under the low branches of the fir trees. Many of the smaller elk curled in an oval, or rather, more of an egg-shape, their rumps forming the fatter end. Their hind legs and fore made tight twenty-five-degree angles bent under their bellies; their faces lay along the narrower curve of the egg shape, and I can even see where they had folded their ears back along the line of their skulls, so completely compact had they made their bodies for sleep. They had not clustered close to each other for warmth, as I might have imagined, but lay separate in the snow, as little as five feet and as much as fifteen feet apart, which seems terribly lonely to me, who have slept in the snow often enough to know the estrangement one feels during the long winter night.

I leave the trail above their beds—the trail cold now with blades of hoar frost settled to the bottom of their prints deep in the drifted snow, where they had come down the ridge at dusk the night before, moments before they lay down to sleep. I leave the trail and cut through the timber toward the meadow where I saw the elk last weekend, but again, no fresh sign. In their place I find only the tracks of a mouse (a hopping two-step with its tail dragging behind) who made a circle in the snow, returning in the direction he came from originally, though nothing in the snow explains why he came in the first place, looked out across the meadow and turned back. Circling the meadow, I find neither coyote nor fox tracks. Perhaps the shadow of a hawk passed over the meadow? Or if at night, the mouse suspected the owl perched nearby? Perhaps it is a thoughtful creature, though most likely, it is a silly one, and the joke is on me, the only laughably thoughtful creature in the meadow today.

Billows of snow poured out of the trees towards me, rolling and blustering not unlike clouds of pollen in July that burst from pine trees at the precise instant the trees know they must make love with the others like themselves downwind. A joyful affection streaming across the warm meadows. But not today, exactly; rather, only this vague resemblance, wind's rehearsal of that form of lovemaking.

ℒℒ

Louis Dick spoke last night at the Middle School. He was supposed to talk about the local tribal relation to salmon, and in a sense he did, though he never said anything specifically about salmon. He talked about death. He made it clear that our actions in this life determine "how to get to the other world," and how all living things—and he seemed to assume that all things are animate and conscious—provide us with the knowledge about how to live our lives properly, and thus lead us to the next world. He spoke about dying and death in a confident and joyous way that was a little disarming if you came to his talk hoping to hear him speak about how evil the practices of ranchers, loggers, and farmers are, as some in the audience indicated was their hope.

Dick spoke about the Law of the First Kill, how a good hunter is always expected to share his first, and perhaps second or third kill (if he is a particularly gifted hunter), with a family that has no hunter. That kind of generosity codified as "Law" seems a perfect way to safeguard against the meanness of the man who throws away what he kills; it insures the exchange of humility and love between hunter and hunted, between hunter and community. In the question and answer period after his talk a number of people asked how they, too, could "become Indians." Several Anglos actually gave their "Indian names." I thought he had said all he had to on such matters. Goodwill, generosity, kindness—that is the way. He had talked about the proper way to hunt deer and elk. That is what he had to tell us about salmon.

⚔

There were places in the snow today where it seemed a bleeding elk had laid down. Faint splotches of blood. Nearby were two sets of snowshoe tracks. I figured someone was tracking an unbred cow elk, as Bruce had explained that the blood only indicates an unbred female. There are so few mature bulls remaining (they, of course, are prized by trophy hunters) and the young bulls are so hapless in their ability to successfully mate with the females when they are in estrus that many of the females remain unbred. I crossed a fence line below the last gate on 12th Street and headed up into the trees. About one hundred yards later, I intersected the snowshoe trail again, and the blood. It all seemed innocent to me at that point. So I followed the trail another fifty yards when I saw magpies, crows, and ravens flying up indignantly into the trees, saying, "It's ours. We were here first. Leave it alone." And sure enough, there in the snow, a recent kill, a cow, her head tossed into the snow, tongue lolled to one side, lips opens, teeth in two neat rows. A pile of viscera. An incredible-looking windpipe, whitish, wide, and symmetrical like a piece of flexible metal tubing.

I circled around it and could see coyote tracks that had arrived from all directions to drag away bits and pieces of the carcass, though much of the animal remained. The right eye glistened with snowlight. There was a set of snowshoe tracks coming in from the east, another from the northwest. The hunters had flushed the cow up the draw and backed her into this deep snow, where, exhausted, she turned to meet her pursuers.

I looked around and found the legs tossed aside in the snow. Each leg was neatly sawed off. At least they had not wasted any meat.

Several other elk had come by to look at the remains, which started me thinking about the possibility that elk may be curious about the death of one of their own, or that they may possess enough affection for one another as to grieve. Imagine finding one of your own kind butchered in the snow. Imagine finding your child. Or anyone you recognize. Perhaps we are used to such horrors. Perhaps we half-expect such things to occur. And perhaps the elk feel the same way. They may, for all I know, acknowledge the grim deed and go on no different than I did. They certainly went on—the herd was nowhere to be found.

Because the hunters who poached this particular elk in the dead of winter took all the meat, one may assume that they needed it, but need often is beside the point. At Thanksgiving last year, our host told us that her neighbor had called them up at the beginning of elk season to offer them an entire frozen elk from the year before. He had not eaten a bit of it, he told them, and was happy to give it away, because he had just the day before "filled his tag," and now yet another elk he had killed was hanging at the butcher's. They declined the offer. "Are you sure?" the neighbor said. "Otherwise I'll just have to throw it away." Our host found the meat still neatly wrapped and labeled in the dumpster in the alley. Such behavior expresses the cruel prerogatives of privilege that many hunters feel is theirs to practice over other beings. In the midst of such plenty, we are starving ourselves to death, destroying our own household.

There are many ways available to us by which we may learn to know these animals. For better or worse, what we learn defies the madness of our Romanticism.

In another month, the elk will have scattered into the hills, where the pregnant cows will begin calving. The deer will have gathered into large herds for their root festival. The first cous will blossom in the hills. Walk anywhere in the foothills and you will smell the musky odor of the plants, the first aroma of spring. And you will see where the deer have cropped the cous blossoms and scooped away the top of the roots as deeply as their convex-shaped front teeth can reach. Look up, and you will see forty mule deer bounding away into the nearest draw. It is the "natural" world as we prefer to know it.

Bruce just completed a helicopter survey of the Starkey elk herd. "Every couple of hours I get sick and make the pilot land."

"You feel better on terra firma?" I asked.

"No," he said, "I just prefer puking on the ground instead of in the cockpit."

Once, while in the air, he saw a group of cow elk gathered in a meadow to calve. The bears, just wakening from hibernation were eager to find some protein. As the cow elk lay helpless in labor, the bears gathered behind the cows and ate the calves literally as they exited the womb. It is not common, but it does happen.

Why is such a thing not painted for the edification of the aficionados of Romantic nature art?

ℒℒ

We have been out along Foothills Road several times in the past month to watch the elk and deer come down to the feeding area. The elk come down off of Glass Hill each afternoon, single file along the game trail from the southwest. There are as many as four hundred elk in all. It takes the best part of an hour for them to descend into the meadows above Ladd Marsh. The hay is spread by the Oregon Department of Fish and Wildlife every morning. The mule deer show up first, eating the tops of the hay, which they prefer to the stalks, leaving the stalks that the elk prefer to eat. A wonderful symbiosis, in spite of the fact the animals are being fed because of the loss of their traditional winter range. I wonder about this. Can it be that, having recognized the negative impact our own relationship to the landscape has on these animals, we feed them the way our grandmothers fed beggars at the backdoor during the Great Depression? Or my great-grandmother fed the holy idiot in her village in Latvia? Has the disaster of our settlement (at least from the perspective of these elk and deer) created a kind of social complexity that invites them into our household as guests? Our troubled and erratic behavior toward these mendicants results from our having not yet fully developed the ritual etiquette that acknowledges our responsibility for their impoverishment.

What is probably the most fascinating aspect of this is that it is a social event for people. Sometimes there are more people than elk. Men lean against their vehicles, steadying field glasses or spotting scopes, each trying to be the first to see the elk appear. Women point to the draw, showing their children where to look. The elk are slow to come down. Sometimes they appear early. They descend in single file from the dark trees, approaching us along the muddy trail that winds through the scrubby draws. Do we interest them? Do they pity us for our hunger?

A student at the local university is "royalty," as she says, from a southeast Alaskan tribe and was invited to the Umatilla root and salmon festival. But she had no ride over the mountain to the reservation, and was feeling very blue about missing this event. I volunteered to drive her, not thinking about how I might be involving myself in a ritual at which my presence could be regarded with some suspicion. Her determination to go, however, was greater than the awkwardness and embarrassment of having me take her. We arrived and she was seated in a place of honor among the women. I, too, was seated with the women (decidedly not a place of honor for men), which struck me as the kind of comic justice I probably deserved. What else did I expect? I was served last, as an apparent afterthought, asked (oddly), "Oh, did you want some of this?" What I was served—camas root, Chinook, and fry bread—

was very good. The meal continued and my companion enjoyed an animated conversation with everyone around her. I remained invisible, but nevertheless delighted by this sudden and emphatic turning of the tables. Wasn't I the beggar at the door now, a guest in this household who must wait his turn, if "my turn" ever comes?

Once I went to buy fish from the tribal fishermen in La Push, and had to stand a half an hour, being ignored, until someone turned to me and said (oddly?), "Oh, you still here? What do you want?" I wanted sea bass, which they sold to me for a price far cheaper than I deserved, and threw in for free a small halibut. Why? Or why not? I held out my empty hands.

When my plate was empty, the two older women beside me at the end of the table turned, smiled largely, and nodding, said, "That's good, huh?" I nodded my agreement and platters came back down the table to fill my plate once again.

After the meal, a bell rang, and a man asked if anyone would like to speak. A small man with long tangled hair, wearing a patched army jacket and torn fatigues, shambled up to the microphone. Anywhere else in the world outside that reservation, this man would not have been invited to the center of attention and given the opportunity to speak; rather, he would very likely be hustled away by the police, and kept out of sight of "decent people." He said, in a voice soft as the April rain falling in the wheatfields on the benchlands above us: "I want to say some words for my cousin, Barbara. When we were kids I lived across the river and she'd swim over there on her big white horse and say, 'George, climb up here, let's go for a ride!' Barbara was always good to me no matter what. She'd help me with bail or food or bring me home from Yakima and give me a place to sleep for a long quiet afternoon, and she'd always come take me up on that big white horse and we'd ride far out into the hills above the river when it is spring, man, and the hills, the hills are all covered with lupine and balsamroot, up there is a whole world of flowers, and my cousin Barbara, who I loved, has gone now and I miss her. That's all I want to say. Thank you."

He shambled away and I sat there dumbfounded, humbled by the poverty of my own language to know and name a world in which joy, not harm, is intended, where every life (perhaps even my own) is a part of a community of all lives, is welcome and necessary.

Gathering: A Calendar

Gathering is older than agriculture and the gatherer knows it.
Gathering is on happier and calmer terms with the unforeseen than
are the later efforts of our kind to control the living world....

—W. S. Merwin

I began scrounging around for mushrooms at the end of April. It has been a cooler than usual spring and therefore a late spring for mushrooms. I went to Montana on the first of May to pick with friends, and was determined to find some mushrooms here before I made the trip over the mountains. It was snowing the day I searched. But I found three fresh grey morels poking out of the snow on the 30th of April, each no larger than a pencil eraser. Incredible to find these three in the entire valley where I looked, the only three (I was certain) to be found, and proof enough, surely, that I could find mushrooms in the higher, colder canyons of the Bitterroots, where, it turned out, I did not find a single mushroom. My misguided certainty about my abilities resulted from my visit to Montana last year in May when I stumbled upon morels growing under cottonwoods on an island in the Bitterroot River. They were very peculiar I thought, because of their yellow caps, the color of old cottonwood leaves. A day later, climbing in Mill Creek Canyon in the Selway-Bitterroot Wilderness I found more morels, and was confident of a repeat performance. But it turned out far too cold this year, and so my dispirited friends dragged around behind me as we searched.

I met two old women on Mount Emily today who had baskets full of different varieties of mushrooms. They had gathered morels, of course, but they also had picked Calf Brains, which must be *Gyromitra gigas*, and something they called Elephant's Ears, which may be a Hellvella of some sort or perhaps a Peziza. They showed me the mushrooms on the ground, but uncertainty persisted later, and I remained wary of picking. I even passed up a perfect, firm, bright group of puffballs, and passed by, squeamish about eating that firm white fruiting body.

The chances of meeting those two women again are probably slim at best. They were old, it is not likely they will be in the woods many more years, and what are the odds of finding them again? What those two old women showed me today, so clear and sensible at the time—"Here," they said, "these, not those"—is little more now than a rumor in my life of an abundance available only to others with greater knowledge and confidence.

ℒℒ

News of shooting in the woods.

The mushroom buyers have set up on all the vacant lots downtown, and late every afternoon the pickers come in from the forests to sell. The price is low this year, three dollars and fifty cents a pound. The competition for mushrooms is ferocious and the picking methods of different groups is causing friction. There are large camps of Cambodian and Mexican immigrants, whose picking strategies vary from the so-called "norm." That is, the Anglos, who have never had competition until now, and use the conventional western pose of the Romantic loner as their preferred style: one man, wandering in an empty wilderness, living by his wits and instinct to eke out a hardscabble existence at the fringe of polite and civilized society, to which he can never thoroughly belong. Leatherstockings. The immigrant strategy is far more cooperative and organized. A half dozen or more men will move through the forest in a line, picking every marketable mushroom in sight. They divide up the profits equally. Needless to say they are extremely successful. And the white guys are pissed off. It is unfair, is their common complaint. Now the white guys are shooting at their competition if they meet in the forest. The recent immigrants are arming themselves, too. Capitalism, its promoters seem to claim, is an expression of God's natural economic will. It is one very strange God whose will these incidents enact.

We pick within sight of home, however, and seem to be well out of harm's way. We have picked a gallon of morels already. Because we have never yet dug camas or cous roots, an activity that occurs earlier in the gatherer's calendar, picking these mushrooms initiates the annual renewal of the year's wild harvest. Dried, these are all we will need for ourselves and to give away for the coming year. They are the first wildness to return to our pantry.

❧❧

For my friends in Montana, disappointed by my failure to find mushrooms on our expedition earlier in May, I now offer this classical form of advice, though the strategies here diverge from those successful methods described just above:

Georgic (For My Friends Who Never Find Any)

*Like the universe, that's how wild mushrooms
grow from forest mold: everywhere*

*is the center, find one erect pileus
and spiral outward in concentric rings.*

*In this way you'll pick all you need
to fill your bucket with black morels*

*any morning in May, when heart-leaf arnica
covers the forest floor in unbroken green*

that ripples like pond water, whenever wind
tires of the pinetops and comes down

to search among modest things
closer to ground. I tell you this because

you'll have to kneel down a great deal,
pray to the mountain's god, who may answer,

booming overhead or pelting you with sleet and hail.
You'll have to get on your knees, peer under

the green shadow of arnica—canopy nearest earth,
someone else's heaven, green sky of a world

always underfoot, trampled, ignored,
very much like the other world you know better.

But here, you visit only during a few weeks
each spring, your giant face reappearing

like a rare planet returned from its eccentric orbit.
Which means you spiral, too, your life

another ring in a pattern of rings with a random
center of gravity. Or there is no gravity

and you are one among many wanderers
wobbling blind through space, until

that metaphor evaporates like sleet and hail
melting back into sun-lit air, and you're just

standing here at the edge of a dark grove
of Douglas firs that didn't fall to a chainsaw,

and right here at the margin between
what was destroyed and what was not,

you clap your hands, laugh, and quickly kneel.

Such advice, followed cheerfully, will be adequate to assure success.

⚘⚘

We were coming down the canyon today when the sharp scent of ripe cherries stopped us. There are chokecherries that we sometimes pick for jam near the gate, but there are also orchard cherries gone wild that line the lower road and ripen a month before their relatives. One feral tree, a Queen Anne, is old, and perhaps sixty feet tall. Next to it is a less prodigious Bing. Both were loaded with cherries. Walking by earlier, we had failed to notice. But this time we feasted. They were not as big as tended cherries, but were more flavorful and better yet, unsprayed. We could reach only a modest amount, but enough to fill me for lunch. The rest are for birds and the bear, whose tracks I saw in the mud after the early-June rains came to an end.

As we were leaving the cherry grove, Josefa said that we pick almost enough wild or feral fruit that we ought to only preserve such fruit and not go into cultivated orchards at all. We could do this, though I objected because it would mean not picking our own small orchard of plums (for fruit soup and for brandy at the solstice), apricots (dried for sweet breads and also for soup), and peaches (in pies and canned), which may be asking too great of a sacrifice. And a foolish sacrifice at that.

But what does it mean to feed ourselves, at least in part, from what is wild? Such a gesture—for that is what it is; entangled in the community and the economy as we are, we would be deluded to believe otherwise—such a gesture begins to reintegrate the texture of one's mind, one's ordinary day, with the peculiar rhythms of the landscape. The relations that then develop between ourselves and a place are complex and affectionate: the community broadens, becomes inclusive, particular, and as intricate an embrace as is possible. Thus, more durable: not surviving, but thriving on sheer abundance.

Until, that is, someone cuts down the wild fruit trees in order to widen the road. So we satisfy ourselves with what we can find wherever and so long as we can find it. We went back up the canyon this evening with a bucket and picked a gallon more of the wild cherries, and making apologies to the absent bears and the misanthropic robins. The feral cherries are drying now in the dehydrator.

♄ ♄

It is strange to think of one's life in relation to a certain number of seasons in a place, taking part in an activity such as gathering. To think now how much time has passed, during which those particular seasons have defined the shape of our lives, pleases me. Half of a lifetime already, gathering whatever we can find to fill the pantry.

Now we are finding huckleberries in the canyon north of town. I checked on them every week since the snow melted off and the shrubs began to blossom. The berries I have seen look large this year, and, given the recent rains, soon should be even larger. This will be the fourteenth year we have picked berries in northeastern Oregon. Last night at dinner, we spoke with a family who had picked many of the same patches as we have, some of which have been destroyed by logging, one in particular on Mount Emily that we stumbled upon a few months before the trees began to fall.

We had just moved to northeastern Oregon, and were driving around lost in the mountains on a road that we really had no business being on in the first place, switchbacking up the steep face of the mountain. Finally, we crested the ridge, and under the old fir trees stretched acres and acres of huckleberries, as big as dimes, and so heavy the branches of the shrubs bent low to the ground. We filled every container to the brim. Given our poverty at that time, I felt blessed by the prospect of a year to come full of pies and muffins and jam. I asked my children, "I wonder what the poor people are doing today?" though they were still too young to understand the irony of it.

By the next year all that wealth of fruit had been destroyed to capitalize on the wealth of trees. Today, fourteen summers later, that ridge is still a stumpland of thistles seared brown each summer by the sun.

❧❧

We picked in the canyon today. This is where we always begin, working our way north, and toward higher altitudes through the end of August, when we'll join many families (often of several generations) of huckleberry pickers near Ruckle Junction. Then it will be time for "Huckles at Ruckles," we say, indicating that the season has reached its height.

Often in the West we meet people who are annoyed to be in the presence of so many others. This is evident during summer holidays in the high country, when urban people travel here for their "wilderness experience" and are disappointed, if not outright hostile, to find that there are many people who share their interest in being in the high country at both the beginning and end of summer. They get grumpy. They had intended to feel like Adam and Eve, but Eden is full of people!

But picking berries, I feel a tremendous gratitude for the presence of so many others—despite the dance rhythms of our disparate lives, all of us in this instance answer the same drumbeat of the land.

❧❧

The first time Josefa and I went out to pick huckleberries must have been in Pattee Canyon in Montana in 1981. By the summer of 1982, we were picking a patch just outside our cabin at the Bear Creek Ranch. It was four years earlier, though, when my friend

Leo and I picked grouse huckleberries (which are to huckleberries what wild strawberries are to field strawberries) on the lower slopes of Wind River Peak in Wyoming, and that became the flavor in our pancakes as we waited out a long week of September snowstorms.

What a mixture of intense tastes in a single berry: a gaminess, sweetness, tartness, and a vague saltiness. That taste was the first conscious pleasure I ever took in gathering wild fruit, though I had picked blackberries with my grandfather. And there is a literary as well as sentimental antecedent to my passion for picking wild fruit. Donald Hall's memoir of picking blueberries with his grandfather on Mount Kearsarge, above Wilmot, New Hampshire. That book, *String Too Short to Be Saved*, and that essay in particular, had an enormous impact on me; it was the book I needed to find at that moment in 1976. I read it in the year following my own grandfather's death, when I was still sorting out those practices of his that, despite our disastrous relations during my late teens, I intended to accept as my own domestic practices, and, I hoped, to pass along to my children.

Once I had eaten huckleberries for the first time in a cool, damp mountain forest at the height of summer, I was permanently infected by a madness for gathering. The finest thing I could imagine was picking enough berries to eat huckleberry muffins once a week for an entire year. For a long time, I held myself and my family to this maniacal standard: fifty-two one-cup freezer bags of berries. I kept count by making sure that everyone used a half-cup container and we counted one through one hundred and four. Once we reached that point, I would relent and pick berries for jam, pies, brandy, and vinegar. And then for the entire year, I made muffins every weekend. I am not as insistent as I once was, although the ideal remains: an abundance of huckleberries, the joy of huckleberries, is the truest sign of wealth.

It is not such a bit of insane routine as one might think, year in year out, picking enough huckleberries to permit a weekly ration.

Huckleberries are the predominate—"most constant," botanist Charles Johnson calls them—wild fruit in the mountains of northeastern Oregon. Huckleberries were the primary summer food gathered by the Nez Perce, and as such the berries have been picked, in the same places as we pick, for thousands of years. Picking berries is one of the few activities we engage in that provides us with even the most oblique glimpse of the vertical depth of presence across generations that have existed here. Gathering assures us an anonymous place in that ancient practice.

As one picks, one is present, here and now, though one also is aware of some concurrent dreamtime that envelops the present. Picking berries, like occupying old houses, is only a moment really in the enduring presence of the berry patch (or that house), which accumulates lives, and thus possesses a force of life greater than any single individual's life. To wish to indulge in the sweetness of this fact every week of the year may be madness, but it is also divinest sense.

ℒℒ

For the first time, our oldest son has picked huckleberries with his friends. I would regret his absence from our family's picking ritual—and for the very practical reason that he is a focused and fast picker—except that he and his friends are carrying on into a new generation an activity they value. We have been invited to their camp tonight for huckleberry flambé. "Uh . . . could you bring . . . uh . . . the brandy, and uh, the ice cream," he said from a cell phone.

ℒℒ

There are others here, too, besides the human citizens of northeastern Oregon, and their stories accumulate alongside ours. There are bears, of course, whose primary summer food is huckleberries, and we often end up having to share a patch, or just as likely, move on to another when a bear stakes its claim to the choicest. They can tell the difference in the qualities of the berries as easily as we can and they are as likely to high-grade the shrubs as we are.

When our son Ezra was five years old, we were hiking down into the Little Minam River drainage to pick berries, and from the moment we set foot on the trail, he began saying, "Oh, there's a bear!" We became angry, told him to stop it, told him (twice) the entire story of "The Boy Who Cried Wolf" (as if that would explain anything!), and still he persisted. Our older son and I went ahead in the river bottom, and passed through a thicket of alders into a huge berry patch. We saw, just to our left, the shadow of what seemed to be a large bird passing over the berries. We looked up. No bird. We looked down. The bear now was standing up on its hind legs, and, terrified by the sight of us, tore off in horror through the alders, just as those behind us were entering the same thicket of alders.

"Bear! Bear!" we screamed.

Josefa, sick of this, and not happy to have been left behind with our "bear-crying" youngest son, began to tell us to "Shut the hell—" when she came face to face with the bear. "Bear!" she yelled.

The bear was now doubly annoyed, and crashed off into the trees up Dobbin Creek as fast as its hind legs could push. The upshot of this has been that Ezra, stunned by his tête-à-tête with the bear, has never since "cried Bear," so to speak. We enter berry patches now, too, with the bears in mind, and quietly share the patch.

♪♪

In one of our favorite patches, it is necessary to pick before the domestic sheep graze the area. The sheep move through fast, but they strip and trample the entire understory of the forest, and their droppings attract hordes of flies. One year, however, as we picked we came across a shepherd who was sitting on a stump at some distance from us, smoking a cigarette. I went up to him to say hello, and discovered he was Chinese, and spoke not a word of English. I gestured for him to wait, bowing and repeating the one word in Chinese I know, "shih-shih," then went to find Josefa, who, as luck would have it, speaks Mandarin. What a shock it was to this young man to have someone, someone with red hair no less, speak to him in an almost recognizable dialect of his own language. He had been alone in the mountains for over a month, he thought, and had only recently begun to see people coming to pick berries, though he was uncertain about the berries himself, and was afraid to eat them. He had been afraid, too, of the bears. After being recruited in China to shepherd for the season in Oregon, he had not spoken to another person since he arrived here and was dropped off in the mountains. He said that he was lonely and looked forward to returning home. All the while we spoke with him, we kept laughing at the improbability of the situation. Although I imagine that many shepherds have been in his circumstances here in the past one hundred years, caught alone between languages—though the majority would have been Basques, not Chinese—each stunned by the violence of the change they had undergone, to feel the rhythm of this land, the dance to which they too were being called.

❧

A few years ago, we came across a commercial picker from Montana, picking where we pick early in the season. We were not rude to him, though what we told him he found discouraging: families pick here in large numbers, all the way from the lowest to the highest-elevation patches, and the high-elevation patches would not ripen for another month. No, we told him, most of the berries here are the smaller, blue huckleberry (*Vaccinium globulare*), rather than the preferred big huckleberry (*V. membranaceaum*). We directed him toward Mount Adams, one hundred and fifty miles west, where he would find larger berries. We have not seen the likes of him since.

About that commercial picker's predicament I am ambivalent: the man was poor and trying to survive in an economy that has no place for him. But gathering is no solution for the inequities of market economies. Gathering exists in an economy older than the market, and is founded on the values and customs of the commons. It is, under ideal circumstances, a sustainable economy. The moment market values invade, much, if not all, is lost. This has happened with mushrooms, which fetch, some years, a relatively high price; though that, too, has changed over time, as one might expect, to the pickers' disadvantage. But market economies are predicated on a kind of violence, competition between those who can least afford to compete against each other, and so must resort to violent methods and short-term self-interest just to survive in the bleakest circumstances. Therefore: armed mushroom pickers. Therefore: root systems of mushroom patches destroyed. Therefore: fewer mushrooms.

Turning the gathering economy into a market economy has one sure result: the joy of the vertical depth of presences in the landscape is erased. That is why the displays of huckleberry cordials and soaps in the checkout areas of upscale grocery stores are so disgusting to a gatherer. The real profit such over-priced novelties produce goes into the pockets of those who never even saw the berry patch from which the berries came. And the purchaser of these products? What does he or she purchase? A feeling of connection to the actual life of a western mountain community? That is about as genuine as believing that buying an SUV gives the purchaser a feeling of connection to the "outdoors lifestyle." The alienation is universal.

My berries are not for sale. And furthermore, I give away my surplus.

⚘

The picking is very good now, all the way across the thirty-mile long ridge. We have picked enough to freeze for pies and muffins, and enough for jam. Tonight we picked our bucketful for huckleberry vinegar and huckleberry brandy. There are many other berries ripe now that we graze on as we pick huckleberries. Thimbleberries are somewhat like raspberries, though they grow only in small clusters on any one plant. Ripe, they are very sweet, and a little bland. Nevertheless, we seldom pass by without eating as many as we find. The same with wild strawberries, which often grow on the sunny exposed banks below the huckleberry patches. The berries are tiny and sparse, compared to huckleberries, but are flavorful and sweet.

We picked with another family tonight, and decided after a couple hours that we had all picked enough now for the year. We drove back down the road from Ruckle Junction and pulled off on one of the hogbacks. We walked out to the rock outcropping and spread our picnic dinner on the rocks, opened a bottle of wine, and feasted on fresh bread, fresh pot cheese, fresh roasted peppers, fresh ground tapenade, freshly pickled beans. The desiccated canyons below us grew dark, violet light spread across the mountains east to west, and the line of the horizon glowed deep red, backlighting Mount Hood, Mount Adams, and Mount Rainier hundreds of miles to the west. A chill came on the night wind, a reminder of what season lies ahead of us yet, the reason we pick in the first place.

⚘

One day last week Josefa and I were walking on Glass Hill when she said, "Do you smell strawberries?" I did. In the heat of day they exuded a heavy aroma like a baking tart. We got down on our knees and grazed across the hillside, picking every berry we could find, exclaiming when we picked one that was larger than normal. At one point I began to consider how unnecessary my attention to these berries is; conversely, I imagined what it might be like to depend on such fruit, to gorge myself out of necessity. Of course, I would then be aware of far more edible wild plants. The Piutes, before being "removed" to reservations, moved about the Great Basin of southern Oregon, Utah, and Nevada, capable of identifying over one hundred edible grasses and sedges. And this was but a fraction of what they found to sustain themselves in that "harsh wasteland" of the desert, much of which has been destroyed by the "progress" of our own economic uses. That I possess only a fraction of the intelligence indigenous to this place is just a fact of my so-called economic "independence" from that feast-or-famine existence. Still, we are fortunate to possess even the little intelligence of this place that we do. At a party last week when I spoke of the wild foods that we were picking, a woman said to me, "We live in the same place, but we occupy different universes. How do you know where to find all this stuff?" She's wrong. I know almost nothing.

We did, however, find enough wild black raspberries today (seven cups) to can a batch of jam. The fruit had so much pectin in it and such a low boiling point, it almost immediately solidified when we heated it with sugar. We turned our backs a moment only to find a good deal of it had exploded onto the wall next to the stove.

ᒉᒉ

Our friend Ben has scouted out a good patch of blackberries along the South Fork of the Walla Walla River near his cabin. We picked the berries today, and they were perfect: ripe, sweet, and juicy, but still firm. After a month of picking huckleberries, it is a relief to be able to pick such a massive quantity of berries in a short period of time. The briar patches in the meadows along the river are immense and many. We picked five gallons in one patch alone and in less than an hour. Our sons were delirious. It was easy to fill their buckets, and they laughed like maniacs as they picked. Because northeastern Oregon is at high elevation and cold in the winter, it is not always a simple matter to find blackberries. Those who live in western Oregon might find this very hard to understand, as blackberries are ubiquitous there. Nevertheless, here they are rare enough, and having a consistent source of blackberries is something to cherish.

For several years we found no blackberries whatsoever. The winters had been harsh and killed the vines we knew to check in late summer. Ben's source therefore has been a blessing to us. One year, however, when an old man in Cove advertised u-pick blackberries we did not hesitate. We called at his door that evening.

He had three long rows of canes, three different varieties—two wild transplants and one thornless hybrid, though it was also tasteless. The berries were overripe and impossible to pick without squishing juice all over our hands, which of course attracted the yellow jackets. The wild varieties with thorns were sweetest. And such sweetness, I speculated, comes from the bite of that thorn. Josefa was flummoxed by getting her clothes, her long hair, and her naked hands tangled in the sharp curved barbs. "I am Santa Josefa," she said, bleeding from her hands and forearms, "patron of berry pickers, and now I am going to the car." I continued, however, up and down the rows, delighted by the abundance, by the cross yellow jackets whose feast I had interrupted and felt I had every right to partake in, and was pleased by the thorns on which I impaled my hands. This, I say, is the ironic source of pleasure—no?

Later, we made a pie, and tasting it after so many years without blackberry pie, I realized that this flavor was the ur-flavor of my life, the first taste I was ever conscious of as a child, a culinary joy returning in the powerful presence of that humble pie.

Picking blackberries is also why I learned to make bread and a good pie crust. My grandfather picked blackberries every August along Sawburg Road north of Alliance, Ohio, at the margins of pastures and woodlots. I sat at the edge of those patches and grazed myself sick on berries as he filled the fruit bucket I use to this day when I pick berries of any kind. My grandmother would freeze enough for pies throughout the winter, but also made us tarts and jam that I ate on her fresh bread. Once I left home, it became my grandmother's last gift to me to teach me how to make the foods she made that I most liked. In letter after letter (sometimes in letters from her sisters and sisters-in-law) she instructed me in the artistry of baking, and when I failed, she provided (again, with the counterpoint of sisters and sisters-in-law) a detailed analysis of my failure. I once estimated that they were providing me with at least two hundred and twenty-five years of combined experience as bakers, and that excludes the knowledge of their own mothers and grandmothers. I open the cupboards, the drawers, and find the smooth, well-worn tools these women used for a lifetime and gave to me because I loved the taste of fresh bread with jam, and fresh berry pies.

My bread, my pies, my joy—these are my tribute to the vertical depth of time.

The frosts have arrived and so we are in a hurry to visit those thickets where the wild plums, pears, and elderberries ripen. The plums dry well and are good in salads and fruit soup. They also make wonderful plum butter, which is perhaps the most beautiful color in all the world, a dark reddish purple. The pears are good for brandy and pear butter. The elderberries make a pie, though only I will eat it. My grandmother always made me one elderberry pie every year. I would show up at her door with the ripe berries, which she made into what is the oddest of pies. Given the many tiny seeds in every berry, an elderberry pie is almost crunchy. Tart and acidic, an elderberry pie is an acquired taste. Hence, the lonely state of my indulgence. My first efforts at making one of these pies was a horrendous failure, and only the intervention of my blind Aunt Tonsi, who scratched out a letter to me, explained how to make this oddity. It is very simple: I had failed to cook the fruit and thicken the filling before I added it to my crust. I was trying, she said, to ruin the pie.

Picking these last fruits of the season is a joy because they are the most overlooked. They have escaped old orchards and grow alongside country roads. We are, at least, eccentric to be picking them. I have no problem with this. Everyone else seems pleased to let the fruit rot on the ground, a fact that baffles me, as my grandparents' generation, who were young couples just starting out during the Great Depression, would be mortified to have their descendants behave in such a way. They have passed away from this world, but the fruit remains, in abundance.

I told my friend George that the older I get, the more tolerant I expect younger people to be of my pitching a ladder into the boughs of feral fruit trees. An example of living memory.

"I'll hold you to that," he said.

❧❧

George called last night and said he was going out to pick feral apples for cider, and did we want to come along? He was depending on us, as our children could be the monkeys high in the branches, shaking down a rain of little apples onto our tarps.

Which is what we did this morning.

We drove to a ranch ten miles north of town, opened the gate to the overgrown northwest corner of the pasture where the now neglected orchard had been planted seventy years ago, spread out our tarps and sent the boys into the trees, where they started shaking down apples. It did not take an hour. We filled two dozen apple boxes (George's grandfather's apple boxes), and came back to town in early afternoon to set up the cider press. It was cold and windy, so we also had to set the ping-pong table on edge to block the wind as we worked. We washed the apples in a large stainless steel tub, cut out the worm-holes, poured these apples into the chopper, then into the press, and twisted it tight hour after hour, all afternoon, watching the juice pour out into the dozens of glass gallon jars we were able to scrounge up from basements and garages. Afterwards, we ate plates of pasta we tossed in pesto made fresh from the remaining basil plants in the garden.

When I was a teenager, my uncle Joe became our source of cider. After coming home from Vietnam, he rented a house that had an orchard behind it, and pressed his own cider each fall. My grandfather, who was not a drinking man, married as he was to a teetotalling Presbyterian, nevertheless made this exception: once the cider "had eyes in it" and had begun to go hard, he relieved his younger brother of the remaining gallons in Joe's garage. Joe, too, abstained, having become a lay preacher. These slushy bottles of cider my grandfather stashed in our garage, in the cupboard where he kept the Black Flag, a can of kerosene, axle grease, paint, and so forth. Opening that cupboard, one was washed in the aroma of death. Since no one else dared go near this toxic cupboard, it was the perfect place to hide his single source of indulgence in alcohol. All through November and December, he would get up from his chair periodically at night and go to the garage "to check on something." Then he would come back inside, sit down, apparently "having checked," and began to belch and fart magnificently, until it was time to "go check on something" again.

Before this, when I was younger still, we drove out to Zurbrug's cider mill in the fall. The mill was one of the oldest buildings in the county, and had once been far outside of town, though by the time I was born, a factory had appeared on the opposite corner, where they manufactured triggering mechanisms for nuclear weapons. The mill was distinctive because, first of all, it was painted apple-red, with white trim. It was surrounded by towering compost piles of crushed apples and apple skins. That smell is entirely gone from the world now, replaced by industrial agriculture, which does not permit the intimacy of a child standing at the cider press while his grandfather speaks with the orchard owner and the mill owner, as they press the year's crop. The air was redolent with the sweetness of frosted, rotting apples. In the next room (the cement floors and structural beams all whitewashed) were display stands Mr. Zurbrug fashioned from rough lumber and chicken wire. These were painted white as well so that the whole interior of the mill gleamed. On these stands were the local honey, cheese, and dried meats. Outside, russet heaps of apple skins and crushed flesh steamed in the cold late-afternoon air. The loveliness of that moment, and the intelligence of those people, is so gone now from this world, and replaced by an antiseptic sameness, there are times when I cannot stand the kind of people we have become.

But it's not quite gone. We made very good "wild" cider with George, guaranteed to give us what George's grandmother called, "the back door trots"—they had an outhouse.

We took home a dozen gallons, George kept eight. I said, "Once it gets eyes in it, it will be very fine cider indeed." We both laughed, eager for it to go hard, so that like the generations we knew before us, we can fart and belch drunkenly for the entire month.

We divvied up the cider, but also the mash—of which I took home a few bushels to add to my compost and enrich the air with that familiar, sentimental stench.

Jardín Romántico

In the garden in April, shovel in hand, turning over the soil, I wonder: how many more new gardens will I build? Or is this one the last? Is this the garden I intend to know more intimately than any of the others I built and abandoned in the past? Questions born of a modern phenomenon: mobility. Or as my brother-in-law, a realtor, takes an odd pride in saying, "It's a fact that the average American moves every seven years." But mobility is another aspect of that sad goal of the mad-corporate-media-mind: the "global sameness" that insists all places are familiar, but only because they seem generic and therefore interchangeable. In such a world, particular knowledge about a place has little or no consequence on the conditions of our lives. In that corporate world, our relation to a place becomes a kind of frenzied staccato; whereas the garden is a meditative legato, a rejection of mad contemporary states of being.

The questions I ask myself each spring are about permanence and commitment, two unironic and unfashionable abstractions; they are about the willingness to face and wrestle whatever dissatisfies, discourages, or disappoints me. I asked again just last week. Contained within that question—Is this the final garden?—exists an implicit desire to reassure myself with the single most potent antidote to the sickness of my mobility. I planted gardens everywhere I lived in the past twenty years. Planting a garden has become the first task I set whenever I move. Forget painting the interior, repairing rain gutters, replacing stormdoors, jacking up and securing the sagging front porch—please, just avoid that loose step for a while. And forget unpacking boxes. Forget it all! It can wait. First, there is this question to answer: Where shall the garden go?

Having honored this claim that habitation makes on awareness, once the garden is built and then planted, how can we ignore its ongoing demands to pay attention? This is the reason I am reluctant to travel abroad, as most people who travel do so during the growing season. How can I leave my garden for a month or for an entire summer? I may be delighted by the spring-fed gardens in Provence, the rice paddies near Cádiz, the wheat, beet, and potato fields that were once the shtelt on the border of Latvia and Russia where my grandfather was born. But to leave my own garden fallow is to admit to dislocation, distraction, or laziness. Or far sadder still: to illness or divorce. What of the flourishing garden in a foreign village? It is a rebuke: a small plot tended by a resident, often without the desire or ability—one, it seems, is dependent on the other—to leave. Standing at a whitewashed wall in the mountains of Andalusia, I look down into a garden that, it is possible, has been cultivated for two thousand years or more. At this moment I wish to exchange, like dollars for euros, my foolish transient status. The chard has gone to seed, but the lemon tree, the almonds, cherries, tomatoes, grapes, and olives—these are still many weeks or months yet from harvest. An old stooped man and a child I presume is a grandchild carry buckets of water from plant to plant. I have no right to claim a place there among their attentions to what is alive and close at hand. When they see me watching them, they neither smile nor wave. They know that, like the rest who stop at this wall, I soon will be gone. Turning their backs, they return to watering their plants.

❧❧

None of my immediate family were remarkable gardeners, although my mother has grown a robust and exotic garden, such as the one behind her former rowhouse in Columbus, Ohio. She transformed every inch of mowed grass into something to be eaten. But that garden was the glorious exception, not the rule. My maternal grandparents were as woeful as gardeners as they were as lovers. Only late in his life did my grandfather grow a notable garden, but he did so at his sister-in-law's farm, to which he would ride his old two-speed bicycle the twelve miles through rolling hills south of town. This was his way of finding peace of mind separate from the woman with whom he could not get along. Is it a coincidence that his sister-in-law and her husband, who outlived both my grandparents by decades, remained, in their devotion to one other, the most generous lovers and successful gardeners? The garden they tended, though, was not more than a dozen steps from their back door. Given their gentleness and attention toward one another and to all things that extended from their union, how could a garden not thrive in their presence?

Another gardener in our family was my great-aunt Margaret— my grandmother's sister-in-law, who lived, until she died a few years ago, in the Civil War-era house on my family's two-hundred-and-thirty-year-old homestead near Kensington, Ohio. Margaret's garden was as exquisite as it was large, sheltered between the house, garage, chicken coop, and a tall and very old hedgerow of lilacs. Last I saw, the garden was gone, no doubt lost to illness and the nearby supermarkets in Minerva. But as a child, I recall that everything we ate at Margaret's table she grew in that garden. I remember the noon meals she served during the first hay cutting. I was very young and did little or no work, but my young cousins and I came to that table hungry as the men. It was no mere lunch she served. It was a feast. I suppose we ate a course of meat, though what I remember eating were green beans (albeit with bacon), corn, wilted lettuce (again, with bacon), fried summer squash, pickles, salted tomato slices, parsley potatoes with fresh-churned butter, cooked fresh carrots and peas, fresh bread and fresh whole milk. Dessert was fresh "mussmelon." All at one sitting.

Only one garden planted by my relatives is, however, so vivid in memory as to continue to animate my own ideas of what a garden must become.

Helen and Phil, my now aging, failing, great-aunt and -uncle, will struggle this year to plant their garden, if they are even capable now of doing so. They have grown, at least until this year, a fine garden on their small farm along Sawburg Road, on a hill overlooking Beech Creek, just north of my hometown in Ohio. It was the first garden I remember. It was situated in the sheltered northeast corner of their farm, bounded by whitewashed outbuildings and fencerows of honey locusts. It was a garden of intense intimacy, as though, despite their long-bickering marriage, this quarter-acre plot was the actual visible image of the potential quality of their lovemaking. Secluded, labyrinthine in complexity, that garden permitted entrance only from the gravel driveway through a narrow gap between the blazing whitewashed walls of the shop and chicken coop. There, on the southwest-facing slope above, were the orderly rows of vegetables—pole beans, tomatoes, cabbage, summer squash, pickles, greens, beets, and corn— surrounded by an annual hedge of gaudy red hibiscus flowers that Phil replanted each year from the sack of seeds he had saved the previous fall. And there, bent down side-by-side in the lush foliage, we would find them, moving without a word through the rows as they weeded or cultivated.

Phil was a stonemason by trade, and a great hill-walker besides. Given his proximity to Beech Creek, he would walk along that creek and always haul home a particular stone that caught his eye. Every couple of days, year after year, he brought back from his walk another large chunk of limestone, sandstone, or a smooth slab of granite, and added it with great forethought to the stone walls and rock gardens that lined the long lane up the hill to their house. On other days, he would dig up a wildflower from the fields or forest and bring it home, where he would plant it among the crannies of the rock wall, and where, a little improbably I thought, the flowers thrived from the light touch of his attention.

There is no question in my mind where Phil's tender attentions originated. If we visited on Sundays for dinner, my aunt—always apologetic, and oddly unable to comprehend the meaning of their lives—shrugged and laughed, "Uncle must have gone for one of his walks." She would then send the youngest (my cousin, Rebecca, and I), to bring him home to table. Down the rutted tracks, past the stables where their appaloosas stood aloof in the midday sun, we danced along game trails like foxes through weedy meadows, waded the ford at Beech Creek, and despite everything else we had heard from our elders about the grim decades before we were born, our bodies still rippled with pleasure. Though we were almost not children by then, there was nothing awkward yet between us, and so we took our good time, distracted, arm-in-arm, knowing all along where to find her strange and quiet father. We did not especially want to disturb him, sitting alone beside the creek, staring at the black stone he held in his hands and would soon carry up the hill to his garden wall.

Phil had been a hero of the Great War, as his brothers-in-law called it, clearly (in their minds, anyway) a different variety of war than the one then being fought in southeast Asia. They told the stories, in Phil's absence, of his heroism in the European and African "theaters." Though his acts of bravery were as many as his honors (in one story, he returned a shoebox full of his medals after the war, telling Patton to "Go straight to Hell!"), they recounted the most horrible only once: he saved his wounded comrades, dragging them one at a time from the line of fire, and then, enraged, preternaturally invulnerable, stormed the machine gun bunker, where he killed his enemy with his bare hands. A fact I could never quite reconcile with the slender, small-framed man who sat quietly for hours on winter nights before the stone fireplace he had built (again, with stones from Beech Creek), petting his cat, a stray whose purr, beside the crackle of the fire, was the only sound in that otherwise silent room. If he was roused to anger, it seemed his anger screwed inward. And surely his and Helen's private lives were more difficult than I could have imagined. Nevertheless, that garden he built around himself seemed like a lifelong project to expiate the horror in which he had participated. It was from that garden, too, during the summer of the steel workers' and machinists' strike in 1967, when our money ran short, that I remember my immediate family was fed.

&&

My first effort to build a garden from scratch, I literally scratched from rock. Our circular garden at the Bear Creek Ranch assumed its shape serendipitously. I began by dragging an unsightly slash pile from alongside a road on the south-facing slope where I intended to build the garden. I burnt the slash with the idea of generating organic matter, though my purposes were aesthetic: the slash pile—a tangle of root wads torn out of the ground, tree trunks, the crowns of trees, all left to rot in a one hundred-foot-long by twenty-foot-wide by eight-foot-high heap alongside the road—was the by-product of a logging operation, an ugly reminder of the violence of heavy machinery that had passed through in a (finally successful) quest to remove all the timber from the surrounding mountains. True, my fire sterilized what soil was beneath the burning slash, but the soil was negligible to begin with, no more than an inch of yellowish mineral soil that covered an endless supply of chips of shale beneath. I burnt the slash on a cold October day when the autumn rains turned to snow. By dusk, a light snowfall covered the cooling ring of ashes, though at the middle, for many days following, the embers of the great fire I had built still glowed.

In March, when the snow finally began to creep into the shadows and then slowly up the slopes of the mountains, leaving the fields clear, a charred circle sixty feet in diameter appeared in the clearing near our cabin. I grubbed this up with a hoedad and began hauling away rocks to the edge of the circle, and then mixed in a year's accumulation of compost. Next, I defined the circle more clearly, scavenging all the materials necessary to build a six-foot-high chicken-wire fence to keep out the deer. I finished the fence by building a gate large enough to drive a pickup truck through, and then wove slats of wood and bare branches into the chicken wire to make the fence appear more formidable than it actually was. But I still had no garden. I had no soil.

I began running wheelbarrow loads of manure a quarter mile uphill from the haybarn where the neighbor's horses had fed all winter. Soon, however, my friend Bob, who I think pitied me (though I would have continued with my own methods), appeared with a 1961 Econoline pickup that we drove into a nearby feed lot, loaded up seven times with rotted straw and cow manure, and then unloaded into the garden. The result, after rototilling, was a very hot soil of manure, compost, and ashes a good foot in depth, which we further deepened by piling it up into raised beds. The entire process of constructing the garden, begun in October, came to a conclusion in late April, just a week before the expected birth of our first child. There is a photograph of very pregnant Josefa, still dressed for the Montana cold, using a hoe to open a furrow for beans. Despite the lingering chill, the soil was warm enough to germinate seeds and create its own microclimate to ward off the dawn frost that would often lie in a white ring around the otherwise steaming garden.

Believing in the sympathetic relations between the shape of the garden and its potential for actually growing vegetables, we laid out the beds in the shape of the Chinese character for "life," *ch'i*. Each "brush stroke" was a raised bed. And the garden was productive by the standards of northern Montana. We grew the usual cold-weather crops (all summer long, of course)—sno-peas, chard, cabbage, green onions, salad greens, beets, Chinese vegetables—but also tomatoes, green beans, squash, and even fava beans. The latter we planted in honor of my Sephardic father-in-law's favorite Andalusian tapas. We ate the favas cold, steamed and salted in brine, removing the shells with great skill, that is, like a Spaniard, with our tongues. Our only failure was with another Mediterranean plant: the lowly luffa, which we had intended to use as the basis of a product line of facial and body scrubbers for the bath. We would be The Big Sky Luffafery and soon would be rich. With a growing season of 105 days, the luffa thrives in Lebanon, we learned later, not in the northern Rockies. It began to frost again in August, and the fact that we were able to harvest green tomatoes to ripen throughout the fall was, by necessity, satisfaction enough to compensate for the failed luffa crop.

We gardened at the Bear Creek Ranch for two years, the second as productive as the first. No other garden I ever saw was quite like what we made there, and our circular garden became the ur-garden of our married life, though I was unable to imagine at that time how different each garden would be. What is most striking now is the last image I possess of the circular garden, having seen it again after fifteen years: no one had tended it since we left. The fences had fallen. All the organic matter in the soil had rotted away. There remained only the rocky subsoil covered in knapweed, chips of shale still faintly in the form of the character *ch'i*.

And yet, through the spring, summer, and fall of two years, whenever the weather permitted, early each morning I followed the winding trail from the cabin through the forest to the garden to drink a cup of coffee and imagine the lifetime I might spend there. Then I would pass an hour before the others woke, watering or weeding. That made-space, I pretended to myself, would slowly accumulate the richness and intelligence of my life. In that garden, I was becoming conscious of what had eluded me since I was a child. We choose to cultivate and shape a space in which to live our lives, allowing the deliberate and the random processes that occur within that space to form and deepen our intelligence. Or we live disconnected, like ghosts wandering in foreign villages— hungry because the nourishment we seek remains inevitably vague and unknowable. On summer mornings, the thin fog illuminated by the rising sun, the intimacy of that eccentric garden filled me with hope for the infinite (and infinitely good) possibilities I believed then still lay ahead of me.

It was in the circular garden that I discovered the aesthetic I would keep striving toward in gardens. Here was a garden that challenged the basic notion about vegetable gardens, that is, that they are tidy rectangles. I have grown a good number of such conventional gardens, acceding to these basic assumptions about shape, but such gardens interest me less than those that, instead, are oddly shaped. I prefer gardens that adapt to the shapes of the landscape, rather than impose conformity upon it; that create discrete spaces separate from one another, but also in close proximity to one another; and that are lavish, sensuous, even erotic.

One garden that continues to influence my ideas about the adaptive shape of gardens is the one my friends Sandra and Philip have grown for two decades on a mountainside in Montana. Their cabin is on a high bench above a canyon in the Bitterroot Range, and so what soil they have is as limited as their growing season. What is not limited is the large glacial till that was deposited around their property at the end of the last Ice Age. Instead of clearing an area in which to plant a garden (impossible really) they built their beds around and among the boulders that hold the heat of afternoon throughout the night. It is an eccentric garden, adapted to the conditions of the landscape, a landscape that not only forms and informs the garden of that marriage, but is a living image of the visionary quality of the lives that built it.

No garden I have built more resembles Sandra's and Philip's garden, nor has demanded more attention and physical effort, than my current one, now in its eighth year, the twentieth year of our marriage. It is the first garden I built that brings together elements from all the nine previous gardens I have built and abandoned. It is a tiny terraced garden on a small hillside. This garden embodies, too, much of our ambivalence about where we live and have raised our children. The decision to buy our house signaled an intention to remain in this community, from which we had always felt estranged, and, in our minds at least, have always been departing. Since we arrived here at the geographical boundary between the Rocky Mountains and Columbia Plateau, we have been dissatisfied with its cultural conservatism, hostility to outsiders, its simplified version of local history (with its inherent racisms). There is also a self-defeating indifference to the health of the natural and built environments; by local standards, all is as it should be so long as the community's wealth of resources continues to flow (illogically) out of the community into the pockets of distant multinational corporations who regard the area as little more than a colony and to whom the long-time residents are beholden for the few existing jobs. Nevertheless, we have integrated our lives and the lives of our children into the social world of the town, though too often as gadflies only. How could we leave now, as Knut Hamsum once said of the modern condition, without dragging our bloodied roots behind us in the road? Where else could we go without provoking a similar ambivalence? We long ago agreed if we cannot find our way to Jerusalem, we should attempt to build Jerusalem wherever we are.

In the case of the terraced garden, our ambivalence is built right into the design itself: each year our attempt to complete the garden is frustrated by the desire to change and revise its ongoing imperfections. This garden has been the most difficult to build, and although it is aesthetically the finest garden I have ever made, the results (its productivity) were at first erratic and therefore seemed as accurate an emblem as we might have crafted of our predicament. In the presence of this garden, I oscillate between extremes of hope and dissatisfaction.

I began building the garden the day Josefa and I decided to buy the little bungalow, behind which it is situated. We stood in the postage stamp-sized backyard that had been used as a kennel, and looked around at the broken fences, the dogshit, the sickly and untended terraced flower garden, the useless patch of grass. "I see the garden," I said. Josefa said that she could see it, too. Without any more discussion, we told the realtor, "Yes." And without any other discussion about gardens, I began building what I knew each of us had seen.

By October, I had replaced the old fence with cedar, replaced the rotted railroad ties in the terraces with new ties pilfered for me by my friend on the section crew, and added a new addition to the terraces—a dog-leg bed two feet deep that reaches another seventy-five feet down the property line. Also, I had gone to all my neighbors and hauled away their garbage sacks full of maple leaves. I brought home truck-loads of manure and sand to break up the clay, and began emptying my old compost pile—transported from our previous garden to the new one like a sacred cargo—onto the "lawn," the sod of which I had already turned under. We had moved our former garden's plants to our friend George's garden, where we built heeling beds for our raspberries and perennials. On the first of November, just hours before the first snow began to fall, we transplanted everything from George's garden to our new one and covered it with a foot of straw.

That autumn I determined the basic idea of the garden. I would build it in terraces up the hillside, and divide the lower terraces from the upper by using raspberries as a screen. Each section of the garden would be a discrete space, only partially visible from any other section of the garden. Despite my own vision of what we were building, our neighbors were appalled. There is something deeply un-American about transforming even weedy lawns into gardens. I marvel at the lawns large and small that their owners fertilize, aerate, irrigate with precious tapwater throughout the one-hundred-degree afternoons, and mow on riding mowers; then they irrigate and mow again, and so on—a circuit of futility. Mounds of their grass clippings clog up the landfill. Meanwhile, they buy food of questionable if not degraded quality at local supermarkets—a good garden will teach you the shocking difference. I come around to many people's houses and ask for their garbage sacks full of hot, stinking, green grass. They think I am crazy. Sure, they say, haul away my trash! I pour out the grass clippings into my compost, where, throughout the spring and summer, in a matter of weeks, mixed with garden and kitchen debris it becomes the black soil I am trying to create in the sloppy gray clay of my hillside garden. But my compost, like my grubbing up of the soil in my backyard, appalls my neighbors. Early in the construction of the new garden, one neighbor child stood on the hillside above me and called over the fence, repeating what was likely the initial consensus: "Your yard is full of garbage." He and his family, in deference to my brother-in-law's insight about the American zeitgeist, have since moved. Twice.

The spring we planted the garden for the first time was spent fetching flagstones from the mountains. With these tons of rocks, I outlined the garden with an oval bed that followed the lines of the fence and raspberries, creating a ring of beds. Inside this ring of beds, I built several long beds, outlined, too, by flagstones placed on edge. Between beds, I laid down pea gravel paths, and after amending the soil further, declared myself satisfied. But not for long. The garden thrived the first year, but by the second, I had decided to change the shape, remove the interior beds and create two large parallel raised beds, to which I added less organic material than the year before. The results were poor. The gardens were easier to tend, but the soil had returned to clay. Disappointed, I changed the garden yet again, enlarging the gardens by using the space more efficiently, and then added tons of grass clippings, straw, compost, and manure. Where did all the tons of organic matter go? It kept rotting fast enough that the loft in the soil quickly reduced to its former tight, airless, concrete-like clay.

Then the railroad-tie terraces began to "walk" downhill. The ties also stank of creosote in the summer heat. So I began to haul rock from the mountains again, this time with the instruction of my Uncle Phil. I had been home the previous autumn for my grandmother's funeral, and spent part of one day with Phil in his garden. He also took time to show me how to build a stone wall.

By the following spring, I was selecting rocks to replace the ties in the terraces, realizing as I picked up the rocks and then began building, that the bigger the rock, the greater the gravity. The greater the gravity, the more stable the wall. I built a tremendous rock garden wall. And gave myself a hernia in the process.

The rock walls were like a puzzle that slowly assembled itself from chaotic parts. The terraces became a series of asymmetrical beds that wound throughout the entire backyard, leaving only a single narrow path along which to pass. Stone steps lead from one level to the next. Woolly thyme, sweet woodruff, Corsican mint, pennyroyal, and lemon balm grow now from all the crannies. In the beds themselves, Josefa planted lavender, rosemary, sage, asters, foxglove, lilies, and climbing roses. The effect is one of walking through a labyrinthine landscape of hanging gardens and hedges that block the view from one space to the next, and spaces that reveal themselves only partially as you approach them from one of the several gates to the garden.

The same day that Phil demonstrated for me the basic overlapping layer design for a rock wall, he also gave me a sack of seeds of black-eyed Susans. At home the following February, I set out these seeds in trays under grow lights. Nothing survived. The next year, the same. Frustrated, I planted the remaining seeds in a pot in May. Still, nothing. I threw out the lot. And the seeds lay in the compost. Late the next summer, a huge weed began growing from a terra-cotta strawberry planter, and for whatever reason, we did not pull it out. Early in September, it flowered. Phil's black-eyed Susan! I gathered the seeds that fall and started them again in pots, and again the following spring they found themselves in the compost.

It is one of the beauties of this garden that, despite its being a cultivated space, the processes of wildness continue, as though, given the opportunity to seek out a cranny, a corner, any niche that escapes notice, the earth will go wild. The terraced garden provides just such a habitat. Spiders, swarms of ladybugs, snakes, mice, mantises, crickets, ants, frogs and toads (very rare in town, and, increasingly, elsewhere) all find their way into the garden each year. Forgotten plants that went to seed, hidden by the growth of successive plantings of other crops, reappear in odd places. Or seeds blown in from the wildflower-covered hills to the west introduce new plants. And so the garden remains full of life throughout the year, much of it beyond our control. Today, rebuilding frost heaves on one of the stone walls, I looked up into the bed and saw one of Phil's black-eyed Susans hiding under the climbing roses.

⚘⚘

We have left our gardens for the month of June in the care of a friend, and have traveled halfway around the world to Spain, to a small rented villa at the edge of Nigüelas. Literally at the edge. The villa is perched high on the wall of the canyon, and though over the back wall we can see into the formal gardens of the Jardin Romantico, from our patio we look down directly into the Rio Torrente, which drains the southwestern slopes of the Sierra Nevada. The river, though, is silent. After a winter drought, only a few patches of snow remain high on the mountain. At the center of town, there is a large spring, but besides this, there is no water. So it is a surprise, Sunday morning at dawn, just before the sun breaks across the ridge and lights the almond trees on the bench opposite us in the canyon, to be wakened by the sound of running water.

The canyon of the Rio Torrente is remarkable. At the rugged, steep-walled mouth of the canyon is a large abandoned mosque. The entire area below the mosque and above the highwater mark of the river is in cultivation. That it is cultivated is less remarkable, though, than the fact that the fincas are very small and diverse. No farmer seems to own more than an acre or two at most. But each acre of land grows potatoes, chard, pole beans, grapes, almonds, olives, oranges, apricots, herbs, onions, peppers, tomatoes, and god knows what else. Each finca has its own design, determined by the rough geography of the canyon. Several have large round concrete cisterns, but most are watered via the irrigation ditches that run along each row of crops. Each field's intimacy is its beauty. Walking along the dusty littered road in the canyon I am embarrassed to stop and look, though to my thinking this canyon is some kind of agricultural perfection: a form of humane, small-scale, cooperative agriculture that has, for all I know, continued since the time before Christ.

There are voices, too, in the canyon below us this morning. When I go to the edge of the patio and look down, virtually the whole village is walking into the canyon, small and separate groups carrying their garden tools. The irrigation ditches are darkening at the head of the canyon as the water makes its way toward the individual fincas, where people wait with shovels to open their ditches and claim their share. I go turn on the tap, but only a trickle comes out. The spring in the square has been diverted from our houses to the gardens below.

For the next three hours, until the sun climbs high in the sky and the heat begins to rise, the village of Nigüelas busily works its fields together. By ten in the morning, everyone has packed up and begun hiking up the hill into the village. The sound of rushing water stills, and when I turn the tap, water pours again into the sink. Just before noon, the bells ring, and the town's people are again in the streets, heading to Mass.

When I look away from town, south and especially to the west of Granada, there are large industrial agricultural fields, even a few center-pivot irrigation wheels such as are common in the American West. The ritual I witnessed this morning, if allowed to persist, could go on perhaps to the end of time; it is a way of being in the world that is proper to the life this place can provide. Its continued existence is testimony to the fact that it is far more durable in the long run than any contemporary method of large-scale agriculture. But it is also very vulnerable. The economic pressures on agriculture, such as those industrial methods of agriculture only a few miles away represent, spell the doom to these peasants' form of farming. The modern world encroaches on this village (as my suspicious presence here makes very clear), and I can see it all around me whenever I look up. And the villagers know it. They understand all too well the threat to the way of life that has existed here in this canyon for thousands of years. We would all be better off staying put, paying attention to our own small plots of land. Seeing these people in their gardens, I of course am carried away by the (impossible) Romantic desire to join them, and so again, in a foreign country far removed from the rituals of my own gardens, I am reduced to being nothing but a hungry ghost.

Last night, walking in the orchards at the edge of town, Josefa and I came across a large viper that had been killed and thrown across the road. Graffiti on the asphalt warned: "Thieves, if you are coming to Nigüelas, expect no mercy."

The Dimensions of Hope

As a kind of exclamation mark, punctuating either end of the five years I knew George Stubblefield, record high water spilled across the riverbanks and flooded low-lying areas of northeastern Oregon. The weekend in May of 1991 when we met on his ranch in Monument, Oregon, and again during the month following his death in December of 1995, the rivers that drain the Elkhorn mountains—the Grande Ronde, the North Fork and Middle Fork of the John Day, and the Powder—rose past flood stage, swollen by heavy rain falling on clear-cut forests and a heavy high-altitude snowpack. Both episodes of flooding were unpredicted and costly disasters that damaged bridges, closed roads, cut off communities, filled houses with water, eroded miles of riverbank, and left shallow lakes in the valleys months afterward. But what was a disaster for many had become for George the occasion of a hoped-for renewal.

During the 1970s, George had followed the advice of agricultural agencies and ripped out his fences along the river, opening the riverbank to his cattle. The agencies also promoted "cleaning" woody debris from streams and cutting down all native cottonwood, willow, and alder, as well as the introduced species: Russian olive, walnut, locust, and mulberry trees that flourished along the banks of the North Fork. The theory that drove this destruction of the riverbanks is still practiced by many farmers and ranchers in northeastern Oregon, despite its being discredited (even by the agencies that once promoted it): cottonwoods and other riparian plants are considered "thirsty" species that act as "pumps" to suck the river dry, reducing water flows and, therefore, reducing the irrigation capacity of the river—which in turn negatively affects the highly water-dependent crops being grown in what is, without irrigation, a desert.

Drive around the river valleys of northeastern Oregon and you will see the results of such destructive practices. Along Interstate 84 between North Powder and Baker City, the North Fork of the Powder River was completely cleared of willows, which were bulldozed into huge heaps at the middle of the streamside pastures. In the Grande Ronde Valley, along Catherine Creek, one farmer not only bulldozed the willows and cottonwoods from his dike, he lit a match to all the undergrowth, charring miles of streambank, destabilizing the soils and filling the channel (a passage area and former winter rearing area for nearly extinct local runs of salmon and steelhead) with long, sinuous shoals of silt.

Along the North Fork of the John Day you can witness much the same thing. There is little or no foliage along the river above or below the fields George farmed. The riverbanks are cut high, steep, and wide. The water in summer is so warm it is uninhabitable by the few steelhead and salmon that make it through Bonneville, The Dalles, and John Day dams on the lower Columbia, and return to the North Fork to spawn. Besides a few miserable hatchery trout released into the river each spring (that mostly die before August), salmonids and anadromous fish have been displaced by bass—a once coldwater fishery reimagined as the sport-fishing waters of Arkansas. Cattle trails crisscross the cutbanks. The water is slow and murky, with a thick layer of frothy brown film and bright green algae associated with a river high in nitrogen and low in oxygen, that is, a river given over almost exclusively to use by cattle.

On George's land the result of removing streamside vegetation was immediate: after a single winter of cutting and burning trees, his riverbank began to erode at a rate of as much as ten feet a year, until the river widened, grew shallow, straightened itself within the bounds of the levee (built by the Army Corps of Engineers to protect George's house after the 1964 floods) and the far riverbank. Even the levee was beginning to erode. Straightening caused the high water of spring to flow faster than ever and increased flooding and erosion downstream. Upstream, beyond the levee, but at the very head of George's fields, the river began to cut closer toward the hills—poised to ignore the levee and carve a new channel between it and the hills. This would in effect turn the levee into an island in the river.

George came to a radical realization: the agency notion of "streamside improvement" was a variety of madness. His first decision was to remove his cattle from the river, then replace the fence where it originally stood behind the levee, and finally redevelop the water troughs where they had always been in the past: at the springs near his hay barn and house.

The results again were immediate: without pressure from cattle browsing or trampling young shoots, cottonwood, alder, and willow sprouted from the levee. Thick, coarse grasses reestablished themselves under the new trees. The trend of erosion reversed. Several feet of riverbank began to add itself back each spring during high water. Across the river, where cattle still grazed and watered at streamside, wholesale erosion continued to eat away at the neighbor's fields, the river widening, though only in that one direction.

ℒℒ

The May flood of 1991 was like nothing I'd ever witnessed. A terrific rain. A deluge that instantly entered local memory. A defining moment. A measure by which a new generation for whom the Great Flood of 1964 was childhood legend would now judge all other extremes. Where water seemed to have never flowed, small streams pounded brown and wide down the hills, currents strong enough to drag away livestock. Familiar streams that trickled like bright silver ribbons through boulders and grasses erupted in six-foot rapids, or in low spots sprawled across roads. The desiccated hills vanished in ragged clouds and dark, isolated columns of rain. Drought had burned its way deep into the land for eight years, but suddenly the possibility of its ending seemed real, a relief and a delight. All the dry cracked earth seemed to gasp.

In the Grande Ronde Valley, where I live, the river reclaimed miles of its once-meandering channel, oxbows reappeared and backswamps filled again, in spite of corporate farmers' desire to plow and drill these low places with wheat. The basement of my house, on the floodplain of Mill Creek, filled with four feet of water that sheet-flooded down our street when the channelized portion of the creek filled with the slough from logging operations just above town, plugged the storm sewers, and overflowed the city engineer's imagination.

But I was far from the Grande Ronde Valley that day, driving toward Monument, Oregon, along the western foothills of the Elkhorns, where, high in the dark east, rain still fell hard on the snowpack. Along the road into the Monument Valley, winding down through beds of volcanic ash, the ditches ran full and sheeted across the road—red, white, or green depending on which layer of ash bordered the asphalt. When I crossed the bridge into Monument, the Middle Fork pounded at the pilings, debris caught in huge turbulent snags only a foot below the road surface. Pastures along the riverbank below the main street had already vanished under muddy water. As I came over a small rise and descended into George's mint and alfalfa fields, the river had begun to breach a low point in the levee, and his son, Robert, stood chest deep in the river, wrestling an irrigation pump from the flood before its motor fouled.

I ran across the soggy mint field to help him pull the pump free, haul him out of the water, and load the pump into the bed of his pickup. Old-growth ponderosa rushed past us from riverside logging upstream, along with every imaginable kind of forest slough and debris that hadn't lodged in an eddy or behind an immovable snag. Robert said the river had risen several feet since morning and that the gauging station predicted it would not crest until that evening at the earliest, several feet above flood stage. We stood on the levee as a warm shower moved up the canyon into the Elkhorns. We were sodden but excited to have stood in the flood and saved the pump (and ourselves) from washing away.

Though the river otherwise raged in its channel, as it made the bend past us the current slowed, spread gently and not as deeply over the sand and gravel bar. This point bar is held in place now not only by the ubiquitous cottonwoods, alders, and willows, but by young walnuts, Russian olives, locusts, and a few mulberries, all the old homesteader species that George could find to replant. Even at flood stage, we saw a heron, osprey, ouzel, and tanager in the secure thickets that thrive there now along the bank. The river was sixteen feet deep in its main channel that day of the flood, but only knee-deep on the point bar, sifting through thick-knit grasses, shrubs, and young trees, which collected leaves, needles, limbs, bark, and, as I would see a month later, a two-foot-deep drift of salt-and-pepper silt. This rich mix of organic matter and fine soil only serves to promote the return of abundance along just one green, curving mile of river. But it is this single mile of river that defines precisely the dimensions of hope that exist wherever someone among us grows skeptical of the simplified vision of our relations to the life of rivers, and chooses instead to encourage the river's own complexity.

ℒℒ

As I write this, George has been dead two years. He decided during his last summer, at the age of seventy-seven and with only a fifty-fifty chance at best of surviving a few days more, to try to battle the leukemia that had appeared suddenly in his blood. The slim chance of living a few months or years longer were worth the pain and humiliation of his treatments. And, in fact, he made a quick recovery. But by December, the cancer had reappeared and George decided it was time to go, echoing to his doctor, his family, and his pastor much the same thing as he had said to Robert and me in

July when we fished for the last time in the mountains north of Monument—just weeks before he went to the doctors, and learned what I suspect that he already knew. "I'm ready to die," he said suddenly, as we drove over Sunflower Flat and looked out in all directions over deeply cut canyons of the Blue Mountains. "I've lived all my life here, and it's been a good life." He might have added, too, it had been a life that left behind good, if mostly unnoticed, work.

During the month after George's funeral, eight feet of snow fell in the mountains during a week's time. The heavy storms were followed by a week of sub-zero temperatures in the valleys that jammed the rivers and streams with thick ice. Then the cold ended in a "Pineapple Express," a warm, wet tropical storm that lasted the better part of another week and led to catastrophic flooding throughout the Pacific Northwest. The morning the rivers crested in northeastern Oregon I called Robert to check on the flooding along the North Fork. It was as extreme as in 1991: the fields surrounding Monument were submerged, as were many roads, and the bridge into town was threatened by ice jams and debris. One ice jam backed up the river and began to flood the cemetery. As Robert stood in the cemetery, wondering how he might break the ice jam and save the soil from washing away around his father's recent grave, the jam, which had pushed three feet of water over the nearby fields, suddenly broke, and the water roared away in minutes. Further upstream there was no flooding along that same section of river restored by George during the last decade of his life. As in the 1991 flood, the river slowed and its waters dispersed through the bushes, trees, and grasses that thrive on the renewal floods offer.

Others have been slower than George to act on this chance for renewal. That autumn before he died, I listened to a radio interview with one of those ranchers along that same reach of the North Fork who declined to have his river frontage fenced for free. His family, he explained in the interview, had grazed cattle along the river for one hundred and thirty-four years. He insisted that the river conditions today are exactly the same as have existed historically. George more or less confirmed that statement as true to his own experience, though he added that his own memory went back no further really than the 1930s, "when there were already some free-ranging cattle in the river and nobody much cared about how the river might have looked a generation before." The fences that did exist then, such as those on George's ranch, slowed the degradation; that is, until these were removed.

✏✏

What George's riverbank demonstrates is the powerful healing capacity of our actions when we take responsibility for the previous harm we have caused. The knowledge of that riverbank is at least as old as the *I Ching:* "What has been spoiled through man's fault can be made good again through man's work." Those who believe the river has not been degraded over time, who deny responsibility for any negative changes, will simply blame someone or something else. Salmon, to choose only one among many examples, have vanished, the argument goes, because of over-cutting on the forests, mining, climatic change, urban development, socialistic big-government regulation, sea lions, sea gulls, or dams. Take your pick. In fact, there is enough blame to go around. The example of George's riverbank suggests at least one solution is to increase streamside complexity, though this requires a certain amount of self-irony, maturity, and a willingness to act contrary to popular belief.

The rancher who insisted that nothing has changed or needed to change along the river reminds me of a prominent rancher-politician who spoke at a hunting and private land-management forum in La Grande several years ago. There were no elk in northeastern Oregon, he explained, "prior to the coming of the white man." This last phrase was spoken with a kind of religious solemnity, an abiding belief in the divine machinations of Manifest Destiny—a faith still held by those who see the West as, essentially, a lot of wasteland that can only be given value through "wise use," by transforming it into something practical, that is, personally profitable. "When I was born," the rancher-politician concluded, "there were virtually no elk on my father's ranch; today we have a population that has increased 400 percent." It is hard to imagine what he believed he meant, as a 400 percent increase of virtually nothing is still virtually nothing. His clichéd, mythical sense of history aside, what he was really saying is that history is a relatively recent phenomenon, more recent in fact than even the arrival of his own forebears. Because he seems to lack self-irony, the possibility that his father's and grandfather's generations of unregulated hunting of elk drove the creature to near extinction is not even a consideration. For him, history begins precisely at the moment of his birth and, we may presume, ends at precisely the moment of his death. And so I suspect the rancher who would not fence his section of the North Fork of being similarly myopic in his vision of the past.

In our part of the American West, the historical record is very brief. That is particularly true of the Grande Ronde Valley, where the journals of early white explorers and settlers provide only glimpses of a marshy valley deep in native grasses "good for grazing horses and stock"; of Bonneville lounging with his companions, king of a land apparently without people; and of immigrant women desperate to get their sick children to the Willamette Valley. The most precise any of us can be when attempting to characterize the Grande Ronde Valley before white settlement is to eulogize its thirty-three miles of meandering river and approximately forty thousand acres of wetlands. The river meanders were drained when the river was shortened and channelized into the now infamous "State Ditch" in the 1880s. The same fate awaited the wetlands, of which there are only a few hundred remaining acres. There is a discussion underway to determine the feasibility of directing spring flows back into the main channel of the Grande Ronde, even though that channel exists only in isolated fragments. And there is an effort now to reestablish wetlands. But these efforts are not driven by compassion for the complexity of the river or the wetlands that once filled with what must have seemed to be innumerable migratory flocks and runs of salmon and steelhead, but by practical, that is, economic concerns: renewed wetlands are a clever, ecologically benign solution for a local water-treatment plant that operates at or beyond its capacity, and the State Ditch, though it reduces upstream flooding, has increased flooding downstream on prime agricultural land.

There are, however, contrary voices in our area who reject the dominant positions of denial or economic practicality. In one of a number of radio interviews with eastern Oregonians about water resources, broadcast on Oregon Public Radio, the interviewer spoke with Louis Dick, a tribal elder on the Confederated Tribes of the Umatilla Reservation. He made the commonsense observation that old stories told by ancestors and repeated by friends, relatives, and elders provide the only way of knowing a deeper local past. He recalled that his great-grandparents spoke of the Grande Ronde Valley as "The Place of the Cottonwoods," where you could walk the entire length of the river's upper and middle reaches under an unbroken canopy of limbs and shade.

At countywide watershed-management coalition meetings, one of the most frustrating topics we discuss is the lack of knowledge about past ecological conditions in our valley, though ignorance about the past has become a cover for those who wish to do nothing. How can we arrive at a vision of "preferred future conditions" if we have only a vague sense of the valley's former character? The condition of the rivers and streams before the inception of modern agriculture is a mystery further compounded by a guilty concern about how our actions over the past one hundred and fifty years have altered the river. There is still a strong, resistant opposition to even discussing these issues. At one meeting

I repeated Louis Dick's story. One quarrelsome fellow seated next to me mistook Louis Dick's name as an Anglo name, and, believing this was someone with whom he should be familiar but was not, he suspected a fraud, an interloper, probably a Californian. He turned to me and asked, "And just when did this fellow's people settle here in the valley?"

"Maybe ten thousand years before you and I did," I said, which of course explained everything, while it explained nothing. He turned away with a snort.

The Confederated Tribes of the Umatilla Reservation have now begun the culturally dangerous process of gathering into a single narrative the oral and written history of the Grande Ronde basin in an attempt to arrive at an image of "original conditions." Their purpose is to force the question: if we know what the original conditions were, and we desire to rehabilitate the river, just how far are we willing to go to actually return the river to its complex form? Would we be willing to reestablish the original channel of the Grande Ronde River, or to use what may be the most extreme example, to remove Interstate 84 (the region's economic lifeline) from the Grande Ronde Canyon, where it was literally built into the channel of the river?

✑✑

Like the meanders, the wetlands, backswamps, and scrolls, like the upstream spawning beds and downstream rearing areas that once supported strong runs of now-extinct coho and nearly extinct chinook and steelhead, the cottonwoods along the Grande Ronde River, too, are mostly gone, replaced by wide open agricultural fields, where the ditches fill, in some places, four feet deep with topsoil blown from those fields by winter winds. Like George's farmland before his decision to re-fence its riverbank, the land in my own valley, too, is becoming steadily impoverished. Louis Dick's great-grandparents, however, complicate the perception of this valley, provide us with a glimpse of the past deeper than our personal memory, and hand us the terrible responsibility of knowing.

For the dimensions of hope to be reestablished in the valleys of eastern Oregon, a new kind of courage is necessary to imagine change that does not simplify but complicates our relations to the land, to each other, and to time itself. Only by observing and learning from the contrary and self-ironic acts of people like George Stubblefield and the few others like him, and by listening carefully to far deeper memories of this land than those the horizons of our own lives define and witness, will we ever inhabit a land and community that is as complex as that thick-knit canopy of limbs that once shaded these valleys.

The Here and Now

We had lived like exiles in La Grande three very uncomfortable years. The night of the first Seder we attended here, we walked toward the house where the Seder was being held and saw what appeared to us to be a leather-clad biker approaching from the opposite direction along the maple-lined street. La Grande is a small enough town that if we don't know everyone's name, all the residents at least look familiar. The biker was a local plumber, whom we often saw in his truck. We felt awkward in this rural, deeply Christian town, to be doing something Jewish and to find ourselves "caught in the act," as it were, by a gentile. How would we explain this? For we would feel compelled to explain why we were carrying a pot of matzo ball soup, a bowl of charoseth, and several boxes of matzo the Saturday before Easter. What would we say? "Chicken soup, apple sauce, and crackers"? "A re-enactment of the Last Supper"? Compelled as we felt to explain, why should we have to explain anything? After all this time of practicing a minimum of Jewish ritual in the privacy of our own home, like Marranos putting on a mask of "normalcy" in a Christian community, the first time we found ourselves doing something explicitly Jewish, we were going to be revealed and would reveal an entire secret society. Given our anxiety about our own place as self-exiles in La Grande, we believed such knowledge might provide a reason at last to attach to our apparent oddity. As always, we felt, at that moment, torn between the open embrace of our identity and the desire to keep it private.

I am all too familiar with this ambivalence, as I suppose are many Jews who do not live in large Jewish communities in urban areas. And I can provide far too many moments from the family album—some comical, some decidedly not—that illustrate the source of this ambivalence. But what is my identity? According to Chassidic rabbis, who have felt the need to explain this to me, I am not even Jewish. My Jewish father married a gentile. And though the rabbi who married them, Rabbi Goran, was very kind and sympathetic, he said to me recently that the prejudice directed toward my parents by Jews and non-Jews alike in the late 1950s and early '60s, that prejudice became my inheritance and would keep me forever, he said, "between selves." As recently as last summer, a pious young Jewish woman informed me, "You really aren't Jewish," and that her rabbi frowns on "people like you" and does not welcome us into his congregation.

Growing up in Alliance, Ohio, in the years following the Second World War, which was still a reality in our daily lives, I was the only child of an acknowledged Jewish family. Many years later, I realized that many of my closest friends' parents had been identified, in a very dangerous mid-twentieth-century sense, as Jews in Europe, but in the America to which they came after the war, some with tattooed numbers on their forearms, they had let that identity slip into an oblivion of silence.

The consequences of my family's acknowledged history were tangible. I was not allowed in the homes of some of my school friends, many of whom during Lent would not even speak to me lest I contaminate their holiness. At sports practices, athletic boosters sat in the bleachers and baited me as "Jew boy" and "Christ killer." My parents and grandparents were barred from joining clubs and civic organizations. We were barred from purchasing land to build a new house, and were restricted to the area, not coincidentally, near the small college, where other equally suspicious "cosmopolitans" lived. The whole unpleasantness of it led me permanently away from home by the age of seventeen. I could count on my two hands the number of times I have gone back there since, so strong was my desire to eliminate myself from the memory of that community. Because of this early history, until given a reason to feel otherwise, I am suspicious of conservative, religious gentiles who wish to engage in any form of theological discussion.

⁓⁓

Blatant racism and family memories of the Europe of 1930s and '40s aside, there are other, less serious, sources for this reticence to "share one's faith," as I have often been asked to do by Christians. There is the patronizing and often comic concern some evangelicals feel toward their "lost" or "misguided" Jewish brethren who willfully deny Paradise, despite the good intentions of those seeking to proselytize us. In such circumstances I have never felt inclined, when asked, to say I am from a "blended" background. I feel even less inclined to claim I am a gentile.

Once, when I was eighteen and hitchhiking across Wyoming, a family stopped to give me a ride. I climbed into the back of their pickup and off we went eastward into the Black Hills. I had been lonely on that highway east of Gillette. Nearby, but invisible to me, someone was shooting a high-powered rifle. The sheriff had stopped and warned me kindly, I thought, to be gone before he returned in an hour. And so I felt grateful for the ride. Behind us, the first autumn storm hung high on the peaks of the Big Horns. Twilight deepened, and the family in the crew cab kept turning around to glance and grin at me. Soon they stopped again and invited me inside. They began singing hymns the moment we pulled back onto the highway, and continued to do so for fifty miles.

I sensed what was coming then, and was prepared—I had just finished my first year at the university the previous spring—to defend myself with my dangerous, newly acquired Continental ideas. I had been an enthusiastic reader of Camus, Flaubert, Marx, and (God help me) the Bible as literature, newly acquired knowledge I was naive enough to believe would free them from the barbarism of their superstition. Already, I was a sophomore in spirit.

Then, as though it were rehearsed, they fell silent, and we drove many miles before the father screwed up the courage to begin. He turned from the wheel and said, "Steve," the boy next to me, grinning like a half-wit, "is going to be a preacher."

"No kidding," I said.

"We're taking him on his mission to call souls to Jesus."

Glancing at the road, then over his shoulder, he said, "Have you found the Lord?"

I hesitated. This was Steve's big moment, as they were counting on me to be a lost soul hungry for the salvation toward which they could show me the way. I did not disappoint them, although I decided to forego the freshman seminar approach and proudly, even a little aggressively, announced my difference. To my surprise, they did not recoil in horror. I succeeded only in encouraging their interest. I understood for the first time that I was a huge opportunity for achieving the ultimate victory for Christ. We soon arrived in the Black Hills. They struggled in the dark to set up their camper, while I went off under the stars to crawl into my sleeping bag.

The following day we stopped at Mount Rushmore, the Badlands, the Corn Palace, Wall Drug, wherever Steve could find someone to buttonhole who did not first offer to beat him up. I do not recall that he saved any souls. But Steve and his family soldiered on, at times blissful as bears staggering from one hive of sweet desire to the next, unaware or unconcerned about the anger they stirred up wherever they stopped. Despite their failure to witness anyone's conversion, they were satisfied.

People were astonishingly hostile and vulgar to Steve and his family, which I suppose was to be expected. In fact, one hairy biker he approached at Mount Rushmore was on the verge of thrashing him, when I grabbed Steve away by the collar and asked the biker to please, just forget about it, Steve meant no harm. Pessimistic and wary, in an odd way I became their protector, wondering, as people became more and more hostile, if the family wished to be victimized, or as they would have said, "persecuted for our faith," as the early Christians were. There were moments when I felt they were seeking out some kind of horrible personal ordeal to survive.

Though they no longer allowed me inside their cab—I rode all the way across South Dakota and into Iowa in the bed—Steve and his family felt assured that I had seen (by the "glinting light" of my eyes?) the Sword of the Lord in that crucial Hour of Power. Whenever they turned to look at me, I would simply shout over the roar of the engine and slipstream of wind, "PTL!" Their delight in my disingenuous conversion was genuine, and looking back, I am ashamed at my arrogance toward their strangely innocent, if deeply deluded, intentions. They dropped me off late at night in Sioux City along the shoulder of the interstate, the whole family standing in a circle praying for the safety of the Jewish hitchhiker who found the Lord while in their presence. I thanked them and walked down the exit ramp humble as an Essene, stole into a KOA, where I showered, and then slipped away into a cornfield to sleep.

Less innocent was the breakfast I ate a year later with my friend's family before he and I set out on another hitchhiking adventure. As we sat down to eat, my college friend's father and mother, knowing I was Jewish and afraid that I was leading their already far-astray, drug- and alcohol-addled son farther into sinfulness, began breakfast with a prayer I remember to this day. They had written it and rehearsed beforehand, as spontaneity was not a characteristic one would associate with their bank-vice-president's-variety of Presbyterianism. "Dear Jesus, our protector and salvation, bless our son and forgive his unbelieving companion, who has yet to commit his soul to thy loving guidance; bless them so that they remain safe, despite the insult the Jew makes of your suffering and sacrifice on the Cross, so that they may return home; in Your name we pray, amen."

"Amen," I said. "A real aid to digestion."

"You're very welcome," my friend's father said, happy to have made this gesture of goodwill on my behalf. A good deed, and an indulgence of my error.

❧❧

What does one learn from such experiences? To lie? To keep secret? To run like crazy from religious bigots?

Leonard was the pastor at a very remote evangelical church on a hill above a frog-loud, snake-infested swamp near where I was living while a graduate student. I had stopped down to the babysitter's to drop off my sons on my way to work. Usually Diana would be wearing her ranch clothes: old jeans, work shirt, a pair of milking boots. But that day she dressed in full C & W line-dance regalia: Toni Lamas, stretch Wranglers, a pearl-button gingham shirt, and, strangest of all, make-up.

"Don't ask," she said when she saw my face. "You will want to get out of here as Leonard is on his way to save me from my sinful nature." She was then in the ugly process of divorcing her husband of fifteen years.

It was too late. Leonard pulled into the lane in his old beater, and parked directly behind my vehicle. What Leonard wanted, it turned out, was a little more covert than Diana suspected: having written off her soul as personal property of Satan, he wished instead for Diana to permit her daughters to attend services Wednesdays and Sundays, to which request she smiled and nodded that she intended to do just as he asked. Later it would turn out that this was a ploy of her recently pious (though adulterous) husband to gain custody of the children, a ploy Leonard allowed himself to be a part of in his quest to enact the masculine prerogatives of the devout, while bringing wayward souls to Christ. Two birds, one stone.

He turned to me.

"And why don't you join us, too, brother?"

I glanced at Diana, who wanted to spare me this line of inquiry. "Oh, Leonard, leave him alone," she said.

"I'm already very well attached to a faith, sir, at the hips and ankles, so to speak," I said.

"Where do you worship? I ain't never seen your vehicle parked at any church around here."

"At home, Leonard. We worship at home," I said.

Leonard, however, did not miss a beat. "That ain't no way to find proper fellowship, brother. You need to come to church."

Diana offered coffee.

"No, thank you," Leonard said. He stared at me, waiting for me to go on.

"We're Jewish," I said, confessing, and hoping this would put an end to our conversation, as he would then see my horns, tail, and hooves plain as day. I have actually had evangelicals, in all seriousness, ask to see my horns, as though I would be exposing a birthmark. They thought that yarmulkes and fedoras covered the horns. How anyone could be so stupid I can't explain, but there you have it.

"Is that right!" Leonard said, clapping his hands and laughing. "Would you please come to church and talk to us about how to become Jewish?"

What was I going to say to this? In some screwy way Leonard imagined himself and his congregation as Jews of a sort, the Chosen anyway, though he was not altogether sure what that meant, besides the not-insignificant problem that Jews reject what I am sure he regarded as the central tenet of his faith. Nevertheless, that was not going to stand in his way.

"Please," he said, taking my hand.

"That's very sweet of you," I said, removing my hand from his. "I really don't think I could tell you anything."

He was saddened by this and turned to Diana, hoping, perhaps, that she might intercede. Diana shrugged. Then Leonard turned back to me and said, with the greatest seriousness, "I'm curious if you would answer just one question."

I nodded.

"What tribe are you?"

I had to repeat the question before I realized what he was asking.

⚹⚹

That night we attended our first community Seder in rural Oregon, the plumber approached us along the maple-lined street, dressed in his black jeans, black engineer's boots, black t-shirt, and black leather vest. I was full of dread. But soon, I saw his vest was in fact an embroidered Ethiopian vest, and the biker's cap was no cap at all, but an embroidered yarmulke! I laughed out loud. We climbed the steps to the porch together.

We were amazed. It had never crossed our minds that so many people were Jewish. There were perhaps forty guests, only half of whom were Jewish, as virtually all of the Jews present had married gentiles. My wife and I were the only "Jewish couple," a perception of my background that I had never imagined possible. Even when I corrected people—"My father was Jewish, but my mother was not"—the fact that I had married a Jewish woman, and had raised our sons to identify themselves as Jews, somehow solidified my identity. It was a little unnerving.

Besides the plumber, there was the defense attorney, the mailman, the organic farmer, carpenters, musicians, teachers, college students, biologists, hermits. We were from Brooklyn, Cleveland, Denver, St. Louis, Seattle; from Ashkanazic and Sephardic families; descended from grandparents born in Russia, Germany, Greece, Turkey, Lithuania, the Czech Republic. We were children of Chassidim, Orthodox, Reform, and (mostly) secular parents. And there was the unmistakable aroma of matzo ball soup in the air (we would learn that this was Jonathan's miraculous matzo ball soup, to which our own did not compare favorably), eggs boiled in onion skin, charoseth, and the strongest odor of all: fresh horseradish. Children ran in and out of every door. Klezmer music blared from the stereo. After thirteen years of wandering in the rural wilderness of the American West, from little town to little town, to find a Jewish community celebrating Pesach seemed as unlikely as winning the lottery.

That first year we attended the Seder was in fact only one in a long series of Seders held in La Grande since the late 1960s and early 1970s when young Jewish hippies, working as itinerant tree planters, began moving into this small agricultural town. Several guests had long ago moved away to jobs on the coast or in larger cities like Yakima or Spokane, but made the annual pilgrimage to La Grande for either the Seder or the celebration of the High Holidays, each return intended as an affirmation of this countercultural community of Jews. We sat at the folding tables, small groups of us each with our own "Seder plates" (paper plates and cups). Though all the proper symbols of the Seder were present (a mule deer's shank bone replacing a lamb's), an observant Jew might well have been appalled by the makeshift nature of the Seder. And yet, despite the fact that half of us were Christians eagerly awaiting the upcoming Easter egg hunt; despite the fact that several were concerned by the utter pandemonium; we followed the order of the Seder precisely from the Kiddush to the Barech and Nirtza. All of us, despite the differences that might have held us apart in another, more formal context, were sitting down together to recreate the historical event, each our personal flight from slavery, each our journey through the wilderness to freedom, and, ultimately, the affirmation of our community through time.

Our Reform Haggadah from a Sons of Zion Synagogue in Connecticut made a point of welcoming all the persuasions in the room. Though it told the familiar story of Exodus, it emphasized brotherhood, peace among different people, a recognition of all human suffering, and lots of singing—"Go Down Moses," "Dayenu," "Eliohu," and lots of summer camp sing-alongs. It was a long service, full of interruptions, arguments breaking out about changes from the Maxwell House Coffee Haggadah (yes) that many of us were more familiar with. Women complained about the still-too-patriarchal emphasis. Boy-children struggled with their home-taught Hebrew, their fathers making either a noble effort or faking it (like our own fathers had, davening and chiming in wherever we recognized a syllable or two of Hebrew). The women, of course, the actual keepers of yiddishkeit, accurately read the text aloud.

As for the food, the horseradish deserves special comment: dug and ground just hours before the Seder, it was so hot it actually brought tears to our eyes, loud howls of painful delight, coughing, feet stamping the floor beneath the tables. Sandy explained how to achieve such incendiary qualities. "The longer you wait to add ice cubes and vinegar, the hotter the ground horseradish becomes." She had made it while wearing swimming goggles. Also, there were two radically different recipes for charoseth: the bland Ashkenazim, heavy-on-apples variety, that everyone recognized, and someone had brought along an exotic Sephardic version that had no apples, but was made of dried apricots, dates, plums, and almonds.

Though the actual purpose of the Seder is to eat the traditional foods, I would fail, however, in observing the order of the Seder if I did not again mention Jonathan's matzo ball soup, the first course of the non-ritual meal we ate. Anyone who has made matzo balls, knaydlach, knows that the outcome is predictably disastrous: they have the heft and texture of building materials. In short, they are gut bombs. Everyone, too, who has any experience eating matzo ball soup has on rare occasion encountered knaydlach that are mysteriously light as air itself. Jonathan's matzo balls possessed this mysterious and much sought-after quality. What's more, they were rich and flavorful, a reminder yet again that schmaltz, despite its bad reputation, can be the source of an abiding joy. And there is yet more: the broth was sweet, the result of his having used the lowly parsnip as the principal vegetable in the broth. Still, Jonathan insisted, the mystery remained unrevealed. And nothing, he swore, could persuade him to tell us the secret of his culinary success.

And given that our Seder was in the Pacific Northwest, the local wines that made the rounds from table to table were from the Columbia and Willamette valleys—Cabernet, Merlot, Pinot Noir, Pinot Gris, Chardonnay. For each "cup of wine," the entire room erupted in loud chorus whenever the service read, in bold caps, "Drink the Vine."

After the meal, much to everyone's delight, the afikomen, the middle matzo of the ritual three that are part of the Seder, had been, yet again, misplaced. The children, waiting for this cue, began hustling around the house to find it. A dozen kids bumped into each other like Keystone Cops, following one another into rooms, ransacking everything in sight, exiting the room, bumping and jostling, until one (always the youngest) found the coveted prize. Next they lined up for their Kennedy-head fifty-cent pieces, distributed by our host. And then out the door they went to play Kick the Can.

〴〴

Indoors, the dishes were cleared away and more wine appeared on the table. There is a Jewish saying I am fond of: We argue to stay warm. In my experience among many non-Jews, however, arguments are to be avoided because they seem rude, lead to conflict, bitterness, lingering resentments, endless disputes over hurt feelings. So, among gentiles I am disinclined to argue for the sheer sport of it. And yet, I long, on occasion, for the pleasure and passion of an argument that is more a matter of rhetorical play than it is personal. Josefa and I had wandered around rural America and lived so long in the absence of Jews, that this pleasure had faded from our experience.

Recently, I was standing in line at a breakfast counter at an airport on the East Coast, when just such an argument broke out between two male members of the tribe (don't ask me which), one from New York City, one from Upstate. It seemed amazing to me how what would have led to fisticuffs west of the Missouri River was little more than a good-natured, if pointed, disagreement about the rights and privileges to be accorded those who visit the country on weekends and those who have permanently abandoned The City (New York City and environs, of course) for country life. And though they had more or less insulted each other's entire way of life (and taste in clothes!), once their bagels and tea were served, one of the disputants said, "I still believe you are a very narrow-minded fellow, but hey—" (and here he opened and raised his hands in an elaborate shrug) "have a safe trip." To which the other replied: "Yes, yes, you, too." Then they shook hands and went their separate ways! It was something that is, it seems, largely unfamiliar to westerners, and when the same thing occurred at that first Seder we attended, how surprised we were by its volume, its heat, its ironic good humor. We argued about the meaning of the Seder we had just completed. To impose order on the chaos of shouts and laughter, only the one holding the horseradish root was permitted to speak.

Few of us, it turned out, held conservative views. No Zionists sat among us and the conversation turned again and again to the recognition that others suffer today as Jews suffered in the past and that Jewish participation in the suffering of, say, the Palestinians, is as inexcusable as it is a disastrous de-legitimization of the moral authority of the very Seder we just celebrated. Not everyone, of course, agreed with this, though they were soon criticized, much to their chagrin, for seeming to insist that the source of Jewish moral authority is a position of abiding victimhood. "Such a contemporary American delusion," someone shouted, and the horseradish root was passed her direction. "This attitude is useful for fund-raising purposes, but it does little to help resolve the crises that plague divided people virtually everywhere in the world."

This is an old and well-rehearsed dispute, and three years later, it would remain a central topic of our post-Seder arguments, given pungency then by two world events: the outbreak of the Bosnia War and the Mount Hebron Massacre. "How is Hebron any different than what we have seen in Bosnia in the past year?" someone asked. "Why do we sympathize with the Bosnians but not the Palestinians, when they are both Muslim? Is our inconsistency on this point hypocritical?" A young woman who was born and reared in Israel tried to explain the almost inexplicably complex and politicized, high-octane-driven social world of Israel, which would perhaps render our conversation ludicrous in, say, Tel Aviv or the West Bank. In this way, the arguments resolve in resignation; such arguments are merely exercises in ironic discourse.

And another Israeli, agnostic in his practice now, though raised Orthodox in a family of twelve, many of whom still live in Israel and practice Orthodoxy, insisted then on making one point he continues to make on this topic each year: "Our lives are so good, they may have never been better than here and now, but that is only so because there is an Israel. We have to ask ourselves if there was no Israel, or no hegemonic American superpower with which Israel is allied, would we be so privileged to meet like this and speak freely of these things? This freedom was never a given in the past, nor is it a given now."

That night of our first Seder in La Grande our discussion focused on the neo-fascists who were very active at that time, and who lived, if not all around us, at least in isolated pockets not more than a day's drive away. It was their unpredictable and dangerous presence that, at the time, added an all-too-familiar urgency to our gathering.

I would like to believe that such racist boobies are benign, or at worst are so incompetent that they pose no threat except to themselves, but that is not always the case. The recent machine-gun attack at a synagogue in Eugene, Oregon, was very much on our minds then, and the very visible presence of skinhead groups in Seattle and Portland and Spokane, and in northern Idaho, had, at the very least, a chilling effect on all of us.

During my first La Grande Seder, something new in my experience was how the leader incorporated the story of the three children—the wise, the wicked, and the fool. It is a part of the service my own family must have skipped for I had no memory of this, though perhaps because I was so petrified by having to read the Four Questions I could focus on nothing else. That night the leader added a fourth child. Each of the first three children question the purpose of the Seder. The fourth child is the child who has no voice, who died in the Holocaust, and therefore, cannot ask a question. At that point in the service, our own children were encouraged to interrupt to ask questions and the younger ones did. "I want to interrupt," said one. "Who is this fourth child, really?" When the explanation followed, how could the seven-year-old questioner have understood? Even when the explanation was personalized (which is partly the purpose of the Seder), "People from most of our families—your parents' great-aunts and -uncles, Anton's, Sandy's . . ."—how does the child understand this but in the most reductive terms? Nevertheless, the seed of doubt or suspicion of others' goodwill is sown in moments like this and the welling up of sorrows, the catching voices, the glistening eyes, what one feels at this moment is as much for the Fourth Child as it is for these living children, the incipient losses of their innocence, faith in the stability of community, and trust in others.

✒✒

One aspect of our yearly observation of the Seder has been its evolution from the ecumenical Seder we borrowed from the Sons of Zion Synagogue in Connecticut, an evolution that has consisted primarily of elaborations and substitutions meant to deepen and broaden the meaning of our gathering. Last year, Mary, a Methodist minister who married a Jewish man, interrupted the Seder at the end of the Four Children, to say she would like to add a Fifth Child, a daughter, who asks about Moses' sister, Miriam, who cajoled her sexually abstinent parents into intimacy, who then reunited her brother and mother when, as an infant, he was discovered in the bulrushes, and thus insured Moses of his destiny. But besides appearing in the genealogies of Numbers, Miriam disappears from the canonical literature.

The story of how the Israelites find water during their journey has Moses "sweetening" the water named "Marah" in the wilderness of Shur. Moses throws a tree into the water, and the leaves miraculously make it potable. "Then," in Exodus 16, "they came to Elim, where there were twelve springs of water and seventy palm trees; and they encamped there by the water." In the folk tradition, however, it is Miriam who resolves the crisis over water during the Exodus. As the tribes wander the desert, she is able to locate water, and by way of her own miracle, summon it from the ground wherever the Israelites pause on their journey. This miracle became known as "Miriam's Well," and sustained the Israelites through the forty years in the wilderness.

"So, in honor of our mother, Miriam," Mary concluded, "we fill a wine glass with water and place it next to Elijah's Cup." This now, too, is a ritual part of our Seder.

Several years ago, another woman, a visiting artist-in-residence in a nearby community, had heard about our Seder and called to arrange a ride from Wallowa County. Because of the large number of participants that year, we moved to the basement of the Methodist Church. During the service we made our way to the retelling of the Ten Plagues that God brought down upon the Egyptians for refusing to free Israel from slavery. With the naming of each plague, as is the tradition, we removed a drop of wine from our glasses with the tip of our pinky fingers, and left ten drops of wine, one for each plague, on the edge of our plate. At the end of the naming of the plagues, everyone reflexively licks the tip of his or her little finger. An unlikely communion—with what? It is an odd custom, blending the terrible with a kind of uncomfortable humor. At our tables, there is no Zionist pride attached to the fact that God punished the Egyptians on behalf of our ancestors; there is no privilege associated with the suffering of others. It is a part of the service we all look forward to, though truly our instincts tell us the ambiguity of the moment is troubling.

The night the visiting artist was present, she interrupted at the end of the Ten Plagues to ask us if we knew why we remove the drops of wine from our glasses? No one knew. Perhaps just to symbolize the plagues? "Yes," she said, "but much more than that." Removing wine from the glass, and therefore limiting (at least to a small degree) the pleasure that the wine offers, symbolizes the joy that vanished from the world as the Egyptians suffered. Removing the wine symbolizes the sadness God feels whenever any of his creation (not just his so-called "Chosen People") suffers. In other words, she explained, this moment in the Seder universalizes at least a part of the experience of the flight from Egypt. The ambivalence of our feelings seems entirely appropriate: "There's no reason to rejoice when you escape the suffering others are not so fortunate to avoid, even if, perhaps especially if, they are the cause of their own suffering." Removing the drops of wine thus memorializes the suffering of others. Do not even think of pleading ignorance of the ordeals other people must endure.

After that night, we never saw this woman again, and no one remembers her name, though I recall that her Hebrew was impeccable. Her words are now a part of our Seder.

This year, Jonathan, who usually made our matzo balls, died alone in Yakima of diabetes. He was fifty-three years old. Another member of the community has quarreled with a number of people among us and refuses to come to Seder or even return our phone calls and written invitations. Others come and go. And now, this most peculiar phenomenon at our celebration of the holidays: the appearance of Jewish converts. The idea of conversion seems strangely unlikely. One is born Jewish, as one is born black or Indian, sometimes one is blended, but it is not exactly a choice, like the thirty-one flavors at Baskin-Robbins. If it is a matter of choice—then what a choice it is! How does one choose, much less absorb, such a complex history and diversity of cultures? Does one convert to Reform, Orthodox, or Conservative Judaism, as one may move from, say, one evangelical church to the next if the religious community is in some way unsuitable? Does one choose to be Sephardim? Or Ashkenazim? Are converts drawn to the idea of the "Chosen People," as though to be chosen were to be, at last, spiritually legitimate in the eyes of God, better than the common lot? It is rubbish. But the ordeal through which these converts must pass, a series of courses taught by rabbis in cities hours distant from La Grande, is rigorous. One troubling and sad fact remains: these converts float in and out of our community, disappointed, and unable to abide by its apparent lack of strict religious orthodoxy or, as I suspect, charismatic masculine leadership. Whatever they imagined or hoped to find among us—a wise, elderly, kindly, and spiritual rabbi?—we have been unable to provide. We are instead, a community of people from a full range of backgrounds and social classes and religious beliefs. Some keep the Sabbath, most do not. Some speak Hebrew, most do not. We come together for Passover, Rosh Hashanah, Hanukkah, and occasionally for Purim and Succos, but always to celebrate this world, this life, without the maddening focus on the next world that I suspect the converts are accustomed to.

It is an old complaint of mine, this resistance to devoting one's attention to the present world as it is. I was struck by this at my grandmother's funeral, at which I sat, not paying a great deal of attention to the foolish young rabbi, who did not know my grandmother, but nevertheless spoke intimately of her as though he did. "Lies, all lies," I thought. But then a startling little old man limped to the bema. He looked, at first, like my grandfather, who had died twelve years before. I sat stunned by this for a moment, but then I heard his soft, thin voice, and realized that he was someone with whom I would have associated my grandfather, a friend of his, perhaps, at the poker table on Tuesday night? But still I could not place him. I was awash with feeling, but of such troubling ambiguity, I could have cried out in my confusion. Then he recited the twenty-third psalm, the most beautiful poem in either Hebrew or English, and I recognized the man, or more precisely, the voice: Rabbi Goran. I was shocked to find him still in this world, and that voice that had so engaged me as a child, a voice that held my attention like no other then or since. And he was not offering me any consolation in the next life—"I shall dwell in the house of the Lord so long as I live." In fact in his gloss of the poem he warned against demanding unreasonable consolation for death, much less an explanation from God. The mind of God, he said, is a mystery beyond our knowing. And when he recited the Kaddish, I was shocked again, as I always am, that there is no mention of death or the dead. The prayer points the bereaved emphatically toward life and the concerns of the living, toward our children and grandchildren. "This life, like no other," I thought to myself—a line I remember from another poem long ago—that echoes something Jesus said, "Think not of the Kingdom of Heaven—the Kingdom is at hand," which has always struck me as a very Jewish thing to say: this world, this life, is your only consolation. It is enough. Dayenu!

And so new families move to town, others break apart or move away, but each year we celebrate this one life. George and Marsha divorced, and eight people from their immediate and extended families disappeared from these celebrations. But some of the new families have small children. We have lived here long enough to see one and now another group of children mature, finish school, and begin to move on into their lives outside their families and our community. Despite all the change, there remains a core of people who continue to come to our Seder, in fact, the numbers have grown, with individuals now coming to La Grande from nearby towns. In George's absence, my wife, the granddaughter of Chassidim, has become our de facto rabbi, Rebbe Josefa. We have no temple, no affiliation to institutions, only to each other in this place, at this time. Only the here and now.

ℒℒ

My youngest son, who is a little tipsy from the Seder, keeps walking past my chair and, stopping to look down at me, sighs heavily and walks into the kitchen. Finally, I ask him, "Would you like to go outside and talk?" For a change, my instincts about my teenage son are correct: it is exactly what he wishes. We sit down at the picnic table and look out through the ponderosa pines at the town below. Ezra is the most worldly and ambitious of the four of us in our family. A musician and composer, he performs in public without so much as a qualm of nervousness. As a pre-teen, when he first traveled abroad, he seemed preternaturally equipped and willing to speak whatever language he encountered. This past school year, though, has been too easy, most of his classmates too immature and too distracted. He belongs to no clique. He has only a few friends with whom he nevertheless often feels at odds. He would be, I might conclude, disgusted with the little town glittering below him. And this is exactly what is on his mind. "I really don't wish to leave here," he says, knowing that his mother and I often discuss this. "There is enough here," he says, though he feels frustrated with people who complain about being bored. "If you sit inside and watch TV all the time, of course you're bored." He looks out at the valley. "Look how beautiful it is," he says, as though that beauty were universally available to all.

Despite our seemingly endless discussion about leaving, Josefa and I know how fraught with complexities that periodic desire has become. To leave would mean leaving this Seder, of course, and this community of friends. I say to my son, "If we left, elsewhere there would be no one to mourn our deaths."

"Don't be gruesome," he says.

"I mean, to cherish our lives the way I cherish some of these people's lives, the loss of which I would mourn and eulogize. We are a part of each other's stories now." As I say this, I feel my face growing hot, and lose my breath. "It's ironic how this place we talk about leaving has claimed us, despite our wanderlust."

He forgives my morbidity. "We've gone almost everywhere," he says, "and no place is better than this, we'd be no happier elsewhere, that's what I mean. Kids complain all the time about how they can hardly wait to leave this horrible place, but they've never been anywhere else, except maybe Boise. They don't understand that this is what life is, and longing only ruins it. If they leave, they may never be able to find a way back here."

I murmur my agreement but otherwise remain quiet. There's no way I can improve on what he has said. The full April moon has risen over the mountains in the east, appearing to fill half the sky at the moment it lifts across the horizon. The valley between us and the far mountains is illuminated in a cold white light. After a while, we go back inside to finish the Seder.

Soon, we are on the porch again, singing "Eliahu," a breeze blowing off the foothills above us and carrying our voices out over the city. Then Brian, in homage as much to the memory of his grandfather's practice as to the prophet, cries out in an anguished voice, "Elijah!"

Someone among the children standing on the lawn below asks, "But what if there were a pizza delivery boy out here, could he possibly be Elijah?" And so the emotion of that moment passes into irony as so much does every day of our lives. Soon, the adults have gone back inside and someone shouts, "Hey Axelrod, Elijah missed his chance again this year. Close the door will you, we're freezing in here!"

I pull the door shut and remain out on the porch. It has been a lovely day, cool but sunny and until now without any wind. The creeks are running full with snowmelt and the wildflowers have begun to open on all the mountainsides above town. Fawn lilies, buttercups, cous, woodland star, grass widow, blue bells, wild peony, and balsamroot. Soon the valley will be mottled by blue swaths of camas. I can actually see the shadows the balsamroot cast on the mountainside in moonlight. Down the hill, the city lights glitter and in the east, the mountains, still snow covered, glow too in the moonlight. I can hear the children shrieking and laughing in the backyard. It is a night, I suppose, unlike any other.

And I wonder if, next year, we will find ourselves in Jerusalem at last? It is a question I used to ask myself every year, as though satisfaction and happiness were a place one traveled toward. "Next year in Jerusalem," if such a thing is possible, is the metaphor by which we must live. The metaphor is, perhaps, better than the actual city insofar as it is uncontested and deliberately excludes no one. We are inventing our own Jerusalem here in this wilderness. Though, no doubt, at some point that claim is as contested as it is elsewhere.

Soon, my friend joins me on the porch. He is carrying clean wine glasses and a bottle of wine. Dick pours us each a glass, and we toast, "L'chaim!" I look at the label and see it is ten years old. He would have put this bottle away in his pantry the year we attended our first Seder in La Grande. It was Dick and his wife, Sandy, who invited us then. It is very good wine, I tell him, and we raise our glasses again to drink.